Edinburgh University Library

Books may be recalled for return earlier than due date;
if so you will be contacted by e-mail or letter.

Due Date	Due Date	Due Date
3 0 JUL 2008		
- 2 ~~ ~8		
- 2 NOV 2008		
0 3 DEC 2008		
0 3 DEC 2008		

INTERNATIONAL RELATIONS AND
THE LIMITS OF POLITICAL THEORY

Also by Howard Williams

A READER IN INTERNATIONAL RELATIONS AND POLITICAL
THEORY (*edited with M. Wright and A. Evans*)

CONCEPTS OF IDEOLOGY

ESSAYS ON KANT'S POLITICAL PHILOSOPHY (*editor*)

HEGEL, HERACLITUS AND MARX'S DIALECTIC

INTERNATIONAL RELATIONS IN POLITICAL THEORY

KANT'S POLITICAL PHILOSOPHY

MARX

International Relations and the Limits of Political Theory

Howard Williams
Professor in Political Theory
Department of International Politics
University of Wales, Aberystwyth

MACMILLAN

Published by
PALGRAVE MACMILLAN
Houndmills, Basingstoke, Hampshire RG21 6XS and
175 Fifth Avenue, New York, N. Y. 10010
Companies and representatives throughout the world

PALGRAVE MACMILLAN is the global academic imprint of the Palgrave Macmillan division of St. Martin's Press, LLC and of Palgrave Macmillan Ltd. Macmillan® is a registered trademark in the United States, United Kingdom and other countries. Palgrave is a registered trademark in the European Union and other countries.

ISBN-13: 978–0–333–62665–8 hardback
ISBN-10: 0–333–62665–6 hardback
ISBN-13: 978–0–333–62666–5 paperback
ISBN-10: 0–333–62666–4 paperback

This book is printed on paper suitable for recycling and made from fully managed and sustained forest sources.

A catalogue record for this book is available from the British Library.

Printed and bound in Great Britain by
Antony Rowe Ltd, Chippenham and Eastbourne

I HUW

Contents

Introduction and Acknowledgements

This book represents a progress report upon my own thinking in political theory and a comment on the current condition of political theory in a climate of transition. The book should be seen in continuity with my previous work on particular figures in political thought and my recent writing on international relations and political theory. The book is also linked to future work on the political philosophy of Kant, the philosophy of history and international relations. I am trying to change my approach to political theory to take account of contemporary social and political changes and to respond to dilemmas that arise within contemporary political theory itself.

There is, I think, nothing remarkable in this attempt to take political theory in a new direction. Not only are there other political theorists who are following the same path but also it can plausibly be argued that political theory has always been an innovative enterprise. For the most part political theorists have wanted to address the most pressing political issues of their day, so that the momentum for change within the subject has not only come from changes in thinking. Political thinking has also been strongly affected by the pressure of events. My argument in this book is that political theory is now being pressed by political and social circumstances in an international direction. In separate chapters I examine, first, in terms of political theory itself and, secondly, in terms of the developing field of international political theory the implications of this change.

The first chapter, 'Kant and the Protestant Ethic', was presented originally as the Bradley lecture at Boston College, United States in October 1990. I am grateful to the Departments of Political Science and Theology at the College for extending the invitation to give the lecture. The approach of the chapter is strongly influenced by the tradition of political theory in that it focuses on the political ideas of one thinker and attempts to situate those ideas in the context of his time. The chapter attempts to demonstrate how Kant's approach to religion and politics was possibly influenced by his religious upbringing. In the manner of the history of ideas (an approach which has played an important role in one strand of political theory) I try then to connect Kant's doctrines with Weber's classical depiction of the Protestant ethic. This brief comparison is not intended to prove a close connection between Weber and Kant but is rather motivated by the desire to shed further light on Kant's ethical and political thinking. I conclude that Kant's political theory represents a secularization of the Protestant ethic.

Interestingly, although the focus of the chapter is on, what is for political theory, the conventional issue of the relation between the individual, society and state, because of Kant's universalist reasoning we are taken beyond the boundaries of this relation. Kant's account of the Protestant ethic is intended to apply not only within states but potentially to all individuals everywhere. Kant is a genuinely global political thinker.

The second chapter on Nietzsche and Fascism is an expanded version of a paper first given at the Conference of the International Society for the Study of the History of European Ideas in Amsterdam in 1988. The paper subsequently appeared in the conference proceedings. I am grateful to the International Society for permission to use the material once again here. In this chapter the question of the relation between the individual and the state looms large as well. I want here to show that Nietzsche's account of individual life and the role of the state is at variance with that of Fascists. Although there are notorious connections, fostered in particular by Nietzsche's family, the general drift of Nietzsche's ideas is away from fascist totalitarianism towards cultural and intellectual elitism.

In expanding the original paper for this book I have tried to draw attention to the novel aspects of Nietzsche's political philosophy which are not state or nation-centred. Nietzsche is a highly individualist thinker and although the main focus of the chapter is upon the disjunction between Nietzsche's thinking and fascist ideology it might equally be stressed that Nietzsche's thinking is incompatible with ideologies in general. Because of his questioning of all absolute values and his stress on the creativity of the gifted individual he provides little scope for the founding of a mass political movement.

The third chapter was first presented at an international conference in Bochum, Germany devoted to Hegel's response to the English Reform Bill of 1831. The paper appeared subsequently in the collection edited by Christoph Jamme and Elisabeth Weisser-Lohmann entitled *Politik und Geschichte* (Bonn, 1995). 1 am grateful to the editors and the publishers for permission to use the material once again here. The purpose of this chapter is to determine the systematic grounds which might lie behind the approach Hegel took in his essay 'The English Reform Bill'. The problem of the relation of the philosopher to the political issues of his day is a very troubling one for Hegel. I attempt to show why this is so in terms of Hegel's philosophy as a whole and in terms of his Philosophy of Right in particular. Hegel does not think the philosopher should be directly involved in changing the world, but there is a specific role which Hegel envisages the philosopher can play.

I argue that the nature of this role becomes apparent in the criticisms that Hegel offers of the Reform Bill.

The general conclusion of this chapter is that Hegel's view of political reform is conditioned by his assessment of political philosophy as a critical form of enquiry on behalf of those whose legitimate and legal role it is to alter a society's laws and its political institutions. As Hegel sees it, it is not the task of the philosopher to inaugurate reform, but rather it is the philosopher's role to indicate the directions in which change might beneficially occur. Those with legitimate authority might wish to act upon this insight. An interesting aspect of Hegel's approach in 'The Reform Bill' essay is that he does not confine himself to an appreciation of the workings of one state. His essay on the Reform Bill is expressly comparative. He makes no bones about the fact that he is looking at English conditions and problems to illuminate broader issues. In particular, Hegel relates British problems to those troubling the Prussian government and compares Britain to Prussia both favourably and unfavourably. Evidently Hegel's norm for the state in his time has a strong interstate dimension to it.

Chapter 4 was first presented at a postgraduate seminar on Habermas's theory of justice in *Faktizität und Geltung* at the University of Tubingen in 1993. I am grateful to Otfried Höffe for his invitation to attend the seminar. The paper subsequently appeared as a review in the *History of Political Thought* in summer 1994. I am pleased to be able to thank the editors of the journal for their permission to reprint the article here. The chapter attempts to locate Habermas's recent work on legal and political philosophy, *Faktizität und Geltung*, in relation to the political philosophies of Kant and Hegel. Habermas's wholehearted support for radical democracy is contrasted with Kant and Hegel's more circumspect approach to democracy. The chapter also contrasts Habermas's discursive interpretation of law with Hegel's socially contextual account and Kant's a priori conception of justice. The fluidity of Habermas's account of law, based as it is upon his theory of communicative action, unavoidably takes him beyond current boundaries. Although in *Faktizität und Geltung* Habermas is primarily concerned with internal issues of justice, such as those arising from feminist concerns, it is evident that his view of law-making as an ongoing debate has important implications for international relations. International law rests explicitly upon the consent of the parties involved and cannot be regarded as all that distant from the ideal of state law in a democratic society which Habermas puts forward.

The fifth chapter on Democracy and Human Freedom was first delivered as a lecture to a conference organized by the Slovak Academy in Stare Lesna in November 1992. A revised version appeared later in the conference proceedings *Human Identity* (Slovak Academy of Science, 1993). I am grateful to the Academy for its permission to use the lecture in a greatly altered form here. In this chapter I attempt to assess some contemporary conceptions of democracy in relation to my own preferred account of freedom. Whilst I take a positive view of democracy I am aware that it is a political form which may not in all respects harmonize with a satisfactory conception of freedom. I argue that freedom, satisfactorily conceived, has to be given a higher priority than democracy. In looking at democracy and freedom in this chapter I take into account the extent to which models of both are influenced by international considerations.

Chapters 6 and 7 on Hugo Grotius and John Locke are intended to make good a deficiency in my earlier work *International Relations in Political Theory*. There I acknowledged that there was a strong case for including Hugo Grotius in a book about political theory and international politics. But as my main purpose in the book was to show that political theory as classically understood had a great deal to say about international politics I felt there was some justification in leaving to one side Grotius since he might not by all be regarded as central to political theory. Since Grotius's concern in his main published writings was with international issues he represented, in a sense, too easy a case with which to establish my thesis.

In recent years, however, Grotius's standing amongst political theorists seems to have risen. Grotius is now seen by many as an important precursor of Hobbes, Locke and Hume. The argument for his neglect in a discussion of this kind no longer has much strength. Grotius's work requires very little reinterpretation to demonstrate his value as a thinker in international relations. His main political and legal writings are in international law. I pay particular attention to the interplay between the approaches of political theorists and international theorists to these writings. Not surprisingly perhaps, political theorists tend not to go beyond the boundaries of the state in their exposition of Grotius and, as is perhaps equally to be expected, international theorists pay little attention to the internal or domestic aspects of Grotius's thinking. This dichotomy is not in keeping with Grotius's own approach. My purpose in the chapter is to argue for a more integrated account of Grotius's political thinking. In my view, the virtue of Grotius's system is that he draws together the domestic and the international viewpoint. He does this through the medium of natural law. Grotius is therefore helpful in making us see that the boundaries between academic disciplines do not necessarily represent the limits of what those disciplines are seeking to interpret or explain. As a thinker of the early modem period, where the European states of today had not properly come into existence Grotius experienced (and reflected in his writings) a society where the national did not take precedence over the supranational or universal. As contemporary world politics arguably moves in the same direction through the process of globalisation, Grotius's outlook may be of relevance yet again.

The seventh chapter is an attempt to look at John Locke afresh through international eyes. I bring out some of the main features of Locke's political theory, for example, his account of the state of nature and his labour theory of property and seek to demonstrate the universal application which Locke sought for these ideas. I present Locke as a political theorist of the expansion of European society, one whose thinking systematized the process of colonization and exploitation of the earth's natural resources which occurred between the fifteenth and twentieth centuries.

Although Locke was apparently preoccupied with the political arrangements of one country alone in his *Second Treatise of Government* he also presupposes a picture of a wider social and political world which strongly influences his conclusions. Locke's concern with the expansion of European society means that his theory has important implications for the Americas. Locke's theory of property was particularly adapted to the conditions of the early settlers in North America. I suggest that it is not incidental that Locke was taken up with such enthusiasm by many of the American colonists. Locke appeared to become one of the key theorists of the American revolution because he developed a political theory which was universal in scope. Although the political theorists who commentate on Locke do not often regard Locke as an international relations thinker there is a great deal in their commentaries which can be used to show that Locke might convincingly be seen in this light.

I suggest that there is a great deal to be gained in an international light not only from an appreciation but also from a critical evaluation of Locke's political theory. Locke's thinking played a significant role in shaping the current political systems of the world (particularly through his impact on the founding fathers of the United States). Just as the main strengths of those systems are reflected in Locke's thinking so also may some of their key weaknesses. I draw particular attention to the possible limitations of Locke's highly influential theory of property. I am grateful to Geraint Parry for his helpful and extensive comments on an earlier version of this chapter.

Chapter 8 was first presented as a paper to the Hegel Society of Great Britain at its annual conference in Pembroke College, Oxford. The paper subsequently appeared in the Society's *Bulletin* (Nos 23/24, 1991). I am grateful to the *Bulletin*'s editor, Robert Stern, for agreeing to my using the material in a revised and expanded form here. The chapter looks at the role of the philosophy of history in the political philosophies of Kant and Hegel with a view to illuminating the role that the study of international relations might play within a reconstructed political theory. World history has understandably always figured prominently in the study of international relations. In attempting to understand current international politics specialists in international relations have looked closely at past world politics and political systems. A knowledge of contemporary international history has also been considered a prerequisite for grasping current problems of world order. This wider perspective has not been considered quite as critical for the study of political theory. If my judgement is correct, political theorists might have thought it more important for students to have a sound grasp first of their own political system and perhaps also some rudimentary grasp of philosophy. The wider world might then come as a later consideration.

Kant and Hegel are political philosophers who make the connection not only between their own nation's political conditions and their political thinking but also the wider connection between world history and political thinking. Both are markedly progressive thinkers. Kant ties his view of progress to a subjective moral judgement about the necessity of improvement and Hegel ties his view of progress to the all-encompassing metaphysical notion of spirit (*Geist*). Kant's ideal of progress is one that is given expression in an all round way in the advance of individuals in enlightened states; Hegel's ideal of progress is one that is given expression through one leading state or people, albeit that the impact of this state or people is felt worldwide. I suggest that Kant's philosophy of history is better suited to a current understanding of international politics primarily because Hegel's metaphysical presuppositions stand in the way of any attempts at reform in world politics. Kant's view of world history is more centred upon the individual and therefore allows more scope both for the individual citizen and the political leader to affect events positively.

Chapter 9, 'Justice in One Country?' was first prepared as a contribution to a special edition of the Slovak Journal of Philosophy *Filozofia* devoted to British political philosophy which I edited with Frantisek Novosad. The journal volume was published in Slovak (No. 49, 1994) so that this is the first English publication of the essay. I am grateful to Frantisek Novosad for suggesting the idea of the *Filozofia* volume and for agreeing to my expanding the essay into this present chapter. In my view this chapter exemplifies the borderline problems with which international political theory has to deal. The chapter looks at nation-centred conceptions of justice in political theory in order to illuminate the problems of political legitimacy being experienced by Eastern European countries. The collapse of communism has naturally meant that these countries no longer have established official ideologies. In attempting to recreate effective political communities many politicians have been led to argue for, and establish, states upon ethnic and national lines. Slovakia's break from the Czechoslovak Republic was itself part of this trend.

Seemingly, the discrediting of Marxism led to the need to introduce new methods of ensuring an effective social and political solidarity. The Marxist doctrine of class has been replaced by the older and apparently well tried doctrine of nationhood. In this chapter I question whether the nationalist path is a viable way of pursuing justice, and ask whether or not justice is best pursued within an interstate and multiracial context.

The final chapter 'International Relations and the Reconstruction of Political Theory' attempts to bring together the main themes of the book. Here I look first at the key reasons for what I take to be the success of political theory as an intellectual enterprise. I argue that a political theory focused upon national issues reflects the parallel success of the nation-state as a political institution. Modern political theory is for the most part the political theory of the modern state which emerged in Europe from about the middle of the seventeenth century onwards. But I would like to consider whether this success will continue. Is the state in its classical European form here to stay? I consider the possibility that the nation-state as a political institution might already be on the point of being superseded. I think it is too early to suggest with much clarity what might ultimately replace it. However I do wish to consider the implications this development has for political theory. If I am right political theorists cannot much longer insulate their speculations from what is going in international relations. International relations theory is not, in my view, a topic outside political theory but one which might with profit be embraced by it. I provide some examples within current international relations theory to bring home my point. Equally I provide some examples from within political theory to demonstrate the relevance of political theory for international relations.

The essays in this book were written whilst Professor K. O. Morgan was Principal at the University of Wales, Aberystwyth. I am grateful to him for providing a stimulating climate in which to consider the problems with which they deal.

Part I
Problems of Political Theory

1 Kant and the Protestant Ethic

INTRODUCTION

This chapter examines Kant's interpretation of the Christian doctrine in the light of Weber's analysis of the Protestant ethic and Kant's own background in Pietism. Kant commends Christianity only within the context of his critical philosophy. Consequently he rejects any ontological or historical basis to the Christian religion and recommends it as an aspect of moral philosophy. Christianity sets for morality and politics the highest goal of a pure ethical commonwealth which transcends institutional arrangements and state boundaries. The rationalist universalism of Kant's interpretation of the Protestant ethic (corresponding closely to Weber's ideal type) makes it still relevant today, and possibly provides one way of finding a bearing in the post-Cold War era.

In my view, the Protestant ethic made a deep impact on Kant's moral and political thinking. Indeed it is possible to suggest that so deep is that impact that Kant's moral and political thinking cannot easily be distinguished from the Protestant ethic. In other words, Kant's moral philosophy is as much one expression of the key ideas of the Protestant Reformers as it is an interpretation and development of those ideas. Kant accepts fully the changes of emphasis brought by the Reformation in our thinking about religion. He believes, like the Reformers, that a belief based upon authority should be replaced by one based upon personal conviction. Kant also agrees wholeheartedly with the downgrading of the role of the priesthood the Reformation introduced and its critique of the institutionalization of faith. For Kant both absorbs and goes beyond the Protestant ethic. His moral and political philosophy represents a secularization of the Christian ideals of faith, hope and charity. In an important sense Kant's philosophy is an immanent critique of Christianity.

Modernism and the Protestant ethic arise together. The modernist emphasis on individuality, its scepticism about tradition and its desire to make every assertion open to proof goes hand in hand with the revolt of the Protestant Reformers against the theological hegemony of Rome. Although many of the Protestant Reformers did not regard their criticism of Roman Catholicism as having a directly political dimension their lay followers were not slow in making the connection. The criticism of established authority in the Church soon passed on to a criticism of established authorities in society. If we connect the modernist spirit in politics to the demise of received, generally monarchic, authority and the rise of representative institutions, then the Protestant ethic must be regarded as having played an important part in this transition as well. The role played by Puritans both in the English Revolution and the founding of the United States of America represents but one outstanding example of this coalescence of Protestantism and political modernization.

The Protestant ethic also has a deep impact on the process of the Enlightenment. The Enlightenment might almost be regarded as the second stage of the Reformation.The leading Enlightenment philosopher, John Locke, was a staunch Protestant who devoted several of his writings to the encouragement of the practice of religious toleration. The general emphasis of the Protestant Reformers upon the laity developing their own religious faith without priestly intervention also prepared the way for an individual evaluation and testing of secular beliefs. As Kant understood it, one of the main aims of the Enlightenment was to encourage each individual to think for himself.[1] It is difficult to imagine that this stage of secular questioning might have been reached without the earlier stress placed by Protestantism on personal faith.

PRUSSIAN PIETISM

Immanuel Kant's parents were Pietists. Kant's mother, who died when Kant was thirteen, was particularly devoted to the movement and ensured that her son was brought up within its beliefs. Immanuel Kant was deeply fond of his mother and throughout his life spoke of his great respect for her love and humility. Kant was also educated by Pietists. He received his education in the Collegium Fridericianum in Konigsberg, which was from 1732 under the direction of Franz Albert Schultz, a prominent Pietist professor and preacher.[2] The teaching of the Collegium was impregnated with Pietist ideals, with at least half an hour a day devoted to religious instruction and prayer.

Even if Kant had not been brought up by Pietist parents and teachers, as a Prussian he would have found it difficult to escape the influence of Pietism upon his thinking. R. L. Gawthrop in his impressive *Pietism and the Making of Eighteenth Century Prussia* gives an excellent account of the strong influence which Pietism had upon the social mores and political outlook of the Prussian people. Gawthrop regards Pietism as almost the equivalent of the official ideology of the Prussian state, growing in influence and strength as the Prussian state itself grew in influence and strength. Indeed one of

Gawthrop's objectives is to establish 'the causal role played by Pietist norms in the creation of eighteenth century Prussia'.[3] Pietism not only played a 'central role in the crystallization of the Prussian political culture'[4] but also 'was intimately related to a number of early modern Protestant and Catholic movements, all of which had a significant impact on the transition to modernity in their respective societies'.[5]

The leader of Prussian Pietism was Philip Jakob Spener. His main theological and doctrinal work *Pia Desideria* appeared in 1675. Gawthrop stresses that the growth of Pietism in Prussia was strongly influenced by the immense numbers of Puritian writings which were translated from English in the period. In common with many Protestants at the time Spener was particularly worried about the gap which had developed between the teaching of the early reformers and the everyday morality of worshippers. Protestant thinkers give particular emphasis to our present life as a preparation for the afterlife. Present sinful behaviour augurs badly for our future redemption. Of course Spener did not believe that good behaviour in everyday life would guarantee our everlasting life but he did think that present good behaviour was evidence of our possible acceptability in the hereafter. Like most Protestants, Spener believed that in not even providing evidence of our worthiness in our present lives we were giving a strong indication of our eventual damnation.

Spener's Pietism represented a movement towards the greater secularization of Christian religious devotion. As Gawthrop puts it, in strong contrast to the 'widely held attitude of clerical exclusiveness, Spener explicitly called for the realization of Luther's concept of the "priesthood of all believers"'.[6] The observance of religious beliefs represented a historical process for Spener in which improvement was not only necessary but possible. As Spener read the situation in his own time there was good cause for optimism. 'God had foreordained the occurrence of a tangible improvement in the level of truth and morality in the Lutheran Church at that time.'[7] Gawthrop attributes Spener's optimism – which ran contrary to trends within orthodox Lutheranism – to the influence of English Puritanism upon Spener.

Significantly Spener's spirituality and his emphasis upon the rebirth of the individual soul did not extend to a support for mysticism. 'Spener, influenced as a student by the natural-law theories of Grotius was anti-Aristotelian and unsympathetic towards qualitative metaphysics in general.'[8] Spener was little interested in proofs of the existence of God nor in any kind of contemplative prayer. Kant, like Spener, was opposed to any kind of qualitative metaphysics. Kant's *Critique of Pure Reason* represented a devastating rebuttal of any attempts to take our knowledge beyond the realm of observation to the realm of the supernatural or mystical. Kant was also to share

Spener's preoccupation with the conduct of our present lives and our degree of morality. 'For Spener the surest sign of a person's true love for God was obedience to God's commands, especially the great New Testament injunction to love one's neighbour.'[9]

Spener stressed our present-day social improvement. He confidently expected and called for 'a gradual amelioration of the worst social evils, among which he included drunkenness, litigiousness, lack of ethical behaviour in the workaday world and, above all, the widespread practice of begging'.[10] But (like Kant) Spener was not a radical in politics. Spener had in mind a gradual improvement in social relations and not an immediate and complete overthrow of existing institutions. What Spener envisaged was, in Gawthrop's words, 'a step-by-step reform that would result from the repentance, conversion and charitable activity of ever larger numbers of individuals'.[11] A better society would be the product of reborn individuals who would demonstrate their repentant and reformed natures in that process of building a better society. Significantly Gawthrop attributes a great deal of the success of Spener's Pietist movement to Spener's willingness to act as an intermediary, to listen to others, to entertain criticism of his ideas and Spener's clear desire to 'build a consensus for his program'.[12]

Although Kant does not share Spener's religious fervour nor the emotive tone of Spener's call for reform he nonetheless has much in common with Spener's approach. Kant was also a keen social reformer. He also believed that a great deal could come from within individuals to contribute to that process. In his political writings Kant shares Spener's humility in relation to the educated public, demonstrates a great openness in his critical approach and seems similarly to tend towards consensus.

KANT'S PHILOSOPHY OF RELIGION AND THE WEBERIAN MODEL

Immanuel Kant and Max Weber are both exceptional figures in the German intellectual tradition. Kant is a major influence upon modern philosophy and a great deal of modern sociology takes its starting point from Weber's thinking. My purpose here is to take advantage of Weber's valuable analysis of the modern religious consciousness in his essay *The Protestant Ethic and the Spirit of Capitalism* in order to shed light on Kant's particular interpretation of Christian teaching. Kant's religious writings have a strong moral and political purpose. A further object of the chapter is to judge the value of Kant's secularized Protestantism from a current standpoint.

Kant was not a politically active person. By inclination and by conviction he was a dedicated philosopher and loyal citizen. Progress would take place not through opposition but rather through providence and wise leadership. Society, in his opinion, should best be changed from the top downwards. It was therefore extraordinary that Kant should in the early 1790s, in the seventh decade of his life, come into confict with his sovereign Frederich William II over the publication of his essay *Religion within the Limits of Pure Reason Alone*. The event greatly troubled Kant who was able to resolve the conflict it caused him only with great difficulty.

The accusations brought against Kant for the publication of the tract have, I think, a ring to them similar to those brought against Socrates by the Athenian population in the fourth century BC. Kant was rebuked for having taken advantage of his position as a learned authority and philosopher to spread false doctrines and mislead the population.[13] Naturally this is not how Kant saw his intervention. But whatever Kant's views on the matter it seems reasonable to conclude that the King, or at least his censors, regarded *Religion within the Limits of Pure Reason Alone* as an atheistic or near-atheistic work.

The paradox of this assertion will immediately strike those who are familiar with Kant's philosophy. Kant regarded his *Critique of Pure Reason* as removing knowledge in order to 'make room for faith'. In this, his major philosophical work, Kant felt he had demonstrated the limits to the use of reason in its theoretical form. As a result of his enquiries he felt that we could not speak with any conviction about the nature of any ultimate reality from a scientifically objective standpoint. Thus in looking at religion from the standpoint of pure reason Kant could not possibly place in doubt the validity of the claims of the Christian religion. Indeed he felt by removing the basis for a scientific critique of religion he had left open the possibility of maintaining a religion founded upon revelation.

As an alternative to basing religion upon claims of objective knowledge Kant proposed that Christianity should justify itself in terms of practical reason. As opposed to the scepticism produced by pressing reason to its limits in its theoretical use Kant felt that he had demonstrated that reason employed practically required the supposition of a divine being. By reasoning in its practical capacity, Kant means the teaching and research of morality. Morality for Kant is practical rationality and practical rationality aims at bringing about the highest good. This highest good can be achieved only by attaining what Kant calls a 'kingdom of ends'.

Kant's moral philosophy is outlined in the *Groundwork of the Metaphysic of Morals* and the *Critique of Practical Reason*. The *Groundwork* pays attention to the nature of the good will and develops the doctrine of the categorical imperative. The *Critique of Practical Reason* shows how religious postulates such as the idea of personal immortality derive from a need to ground morality. Kant regards God as a postulate of pure practical reason.[14]

Thus the doctrine Kant develops in *Religion* is one that brings out the ethical dimension of Christianity. From the viewpoint of Kant's philosophy the most momentous aspect of the life of Christ is the moral example it gave to the human race. Christ indicated many respects in which a kingdom of ends might be achieved and showed the dangers which have to be faced in pursuing the goal. The historical aspect of the life of Christ is of little concern to Kant. Whether or not Christ actually existed and his life took on the form presented in the Gospels would not affect the vision of religion Kant presents in his essay. Kant demonstrates that he has little concern for formal and established religion. Indeed what he advocates is the development of an invisible church which would go beyond the boundaries of all established Christian churches and possibly all religions. Kant appears to present a cosmopolitan, almost secular, argument which would preserve the moral content of Christianity in the service of a divine rational being.

What probably aroused the anger of the authorities were Kant's doubts about the established churches and his criticism of clericalism. Also Kant's factual doubts about the authenticity of the claims of religion cannot have endeared him to the censor. It seems that Kant departs from orthodox religon in the essay. However, my argument here will be that Kant's mature views on religion reflect a natural development of the Protestant views which he was brought up with and the morality he defends is a powerful interpretation of the Protestant ethic which has had such a remarkable and valuable impact on the development of the western world.

For Max Weber the Protestant ethic was a doctrine and way of life which aimed at worldly asceticism. The focus of the Protestant's thought and action was eternal salvation. No one could be sure that eternal salvation was open to them but by performing good deeds in this life they might avoid salvation being barred to them. Protestants sought God's favour and tried at all times to avoid doing anything which would prevent them from becoming one of the elect. And it is the elect only who are favoured with salvation.

Although this Protestant ethic eschewed all earthly pleasures it was not entirely an other-worldly doctrine. Indeed the major Protestant figures criticized the monastic life. For Luther and Calvin it was possible to demonstrate that you were amongst the elect through your conduct in life. Earthly life was an essential preparation and training for the eternal life. The Protestant ethic therefore made secular life an aspect of divine existence. You could act in accordance with God's wishes in the world. So within the various Protestant churches there is a strong emphasis on individual morality. What stands out for Weber in this emphasis on individual morality, and is for him a vital aspect of the Protestant ethic is the introduction of the concept of a calling (*Beruf*) or vocation into theological doctrine.

Luther regards the concept of the calling as a central dogma for all members of the Protestant church which distinguishes them markedly from the Catholic church. With Catholicism, as Weber understands it there appears to be two ethics, one for the priesthood and another for the laity. It seemed a presupposition of Catholicism that the way of life of the priesthood was superior to that of the laity. Protestantism sought to bring the two ways of life together in a single ethic. As Weber puts it, 'the only way of living acceptable to God was not to surpass worldly morality in monastic asceticism, but solely through the fulfilment of the obligations imposed upon the individual by his position in the world. That was his calling.'[15] In the Protestant ethic there is therefore a more positive evaluation of earthly life. Instead of the Catholic cycle of behaviour of sin, repentance and forgiveness followed by more sin, repentance and forgiveness Protestant reformers attempted to encourage a form of life which saw improvement, the fulfilling of obligations and vocational success occurring at the same time. Luther was particularly critical of the apparent virtues of priestly withdrawal. 'The monastic life is not only quite devoid of value as a means of justification before God, but he also looks upon its renunciation of the duties of the world as the product of selfishness, withdrawing from temporal obligations. In contrast, labour in a calling appears to him as the outward expression of brotherly love.'[16]

The Protestant ethic seems then to see the individual as less subject to fate or to the temptation of sin than does Catholic teaching. In terms of the Protestant ethic it makes sense to have a life plan. Not only should we give rein to our imagination and project into the future what we wish to become, it is our duty to discover a calling for ourselves in order thereby to serve God. We are not challenging divine grace in making ourselves what we want to be, we are serving it.

Of course, as Weber points out, the great Protestant reformers were not uniform in their praise of the earthly vocation. With Luther the pursuit of an earthly vocation was not inconsistent with the acceptance of a role imposed upon us by tradition. Calvin stands out as one who advocated self-mastery and control. The Calvinist, according to Weber, stands ready to create 'his own salvation'. 'But this creation cannot, as in Catholicism, consist in a gradual accumulation of good deeds to one's credit, but rather in a systematic self-control which at every moment stands before the inexorable alternative, chosen or damned.'[17]

There is one particular aspect of Weber's analysis of the Protestant ethic on which I wish to concentrate here and this is his discussion of Pietism. We have seen that Kant's parents were Pietists and Kant appears particularly to have been influenced by his mother's devout nature. In his later years Kant may have shaken off some of the influence of his intensely religious upbringing yet the impact on his character of his Pietist education in my opinion remains strong. Kant's mature political thinking was a product of his reception and transformation of the Pietist creed. Kant was both shaped by Pietism and a critic of the movement.

For the Pietist to act badly in everyday life was to demonstrate that you were not amongst the elect who alone would enjoy God's grace. Acting well did not ensure you were amongst the elect since most Pietists believed that those who were to succeed were predestined to do so. The elect were so chosen by God. In doing the right thing a person provided evidence of his predestination. Without Providence on his side the individual was doomed. Grace could not be attained by worldly means alone.

Weber believes Pietism and puritanism were closely connected movements. He suggests that 'almost all the leading representatives of puritanism are sometimes classed among the Pietists'.[18] For this reason there is little mention of Pietism in England and amongst English-speaking groups since the doctrines of puritanism were identical with those of pietism. It seems likely therefore that the puritans of Massachusetts enjoyed a similar kind of upbringing to Kant.[19]

For Pietists salvation was an intensely practical preoccupation; 'election could not be proved by theological learning at all'. The object of pietism was 'to make the invisible church of the elect visible on this earth'.[20] Salvation was not postponed until the afterlife. Pietists sought to establish communities which could enjoy God's grace now by avoiding temptation and doing good works. At times this appeal to present community was accompanied by expressions of emotion – a religous emotion much to be denigrated by Kant.

The emphasis on the beneficial effects of disciplined work was as great in Pietism as in any of the other denominations. Pietism 'strove to make sure of salvation within the everyday routine of life in a worldly calling'. And, Weber adds, 'the practical effect of pietistic principles was an even stricter ascetic control of conduct in the calling, which provided a still more solid religious basis for the ethic of the calling'.[21]

As Weber depicts the mind-set of the Pietist we get an ever more clear picture of the ethical and religous background to the development of Kant's philosophy. Weber not only employs phrases which might have been taken directly out of Kant's essay on *Religion* but also gives a valuable picture of a possible motivating force behind Kant's exacting moral and political philosophy. Kant's moral philosophy aims at the kingdom of ends in the human world. Pietism, according to Weber, 'led religion in practice to strive for the enjoyment of salvation in this world rather than to engage in the ascetic struggle for certainty about the future world'.[22] In line with Kant's emphasis in his notion of the categorical imperative on the value of the ethical motivation in itself and the possibility of community it indicated, Weber notes that, with the Pietists 'even the attainment of divine grace became in effect an object of rational human activity'.[23]

Thus although the emphasis with Pietism was, as with all Christian religion, the attainment of eternal life, the practical impact of the doctrine was to lead to an intense concentration on action in the present. Pietists gave very close attention to the reform of the individual. In their view, all individuals had the potential power to improve themselves and thereby improve the world. The personal and particular they regarded as instances of the divine. Even if betterment might only be achieved in the smallest details this would be to the greater glory of God. As Weber comments, 'the virtues favoured by Pietism were more those on the one hand of the faithful official, clerk, labourer or domestic worker, and on the other of the predominantly patriarchal employer'.[24] As the name suggests, pietists saw improvement occurring through a devotion to duty in everyday life. But this was not only an improvement within the individual in God's eyes, Pietists also saw dutiful action as bringing about social and political improvement.

In my view the doctrines in Kant's *Religion within the Limits of Pure Reason Alone* follow on from the Pietist creed. They are therefore a development of the Protestant ethic. In one respect, Kant carries to a logical conclusion the Protestant's dislike of outward ceremony, of external demonstrations of piety and stress on earthly duty and community to advocate a secular doctrine of progress. Where the practising Protestant might certainly draw the line is with Kant's preparedness, if needs be, to dispense with the Bible and any outward institutional form. Kant takes the universality of the Pietist creed to such a point that he is not only prepared to enter into community with all races and creeds but he is also prepared to dispense with the church itself. This is a step which takes Kant beyond conventional Pietism but it is not a step that is wholly hostile to the spirit of the movement. As *The Encyclopedia of Religion* puts it, the fellowship of Pietism 'was perceived to transcend every barrier of church affiliation, race, class and nationality – even that of time'.[25] Pietism itself had cosmopolitan implications.

RELIGION, MORALITY AND POLITICS

For Kant the essence of the Christian religion is its ethical doctrine. This ethical doctrine was exemplified in the life of Christ. 'The teacher of the Gospel announced himself to be an ambassador from heaven. As one worthy of such a mission, he declared that servile belief (taking the form of confessions and practices of divine worship) is essentially vain and that moral faith, which alone renders man holy ... is the only saving faith.' In his demeanour Christ opposed superstition, fatalism and unthinking authoritarianism. In his own person Christ gave an example 'conforming to the archetype of a humanity alone pleasing to God'.[26]

In the book *Kant's Philosophy of Religion* Clement Webb concludes that there are three strong points to Kant's thinking. The first thing which Kant points to is 'the implicit rationality of religion'.[27] By this Webb means that for Kant the heart of the religious experience is not emotion or feeling but, rather, practical reasoning. Although Kant does not accept the traditional proofs of God's existence he accepts, nonetheless, that the postulate of God has a rational basis. According to Webb, Kant's second major contribution is to draw attention to 'the implicitly ethical character of religion'.[28] Kant in fact goes further than Webb suggests in that he recognizes as genuinely religious only that which deals with the moral laws of human behaviour. Kant has no time for those aspects of religious practice which appeal to superstition, sentiment and enthusiasm. The third major point which Kant makes is to place emphasis on the 'ethical or ethically rational character of the Christian religion'.[29] What Kant discovers in the Christian religion is not so much the faith in the existence of a divine being who governs the course of the world and life hereafter but rather a code for moral action. The strength of Christianity is to make this code for action a faith in itself.

Kant was led to regard morality so highly by his *Critique of Pure Reason*. In demonstrating the limits to the employment of our theoretical reason Kant was led to practical reason as providing the only full and adequate outlet for our rational capacities. Although reason cannot bring the whole of the objective world under its spell it does have a possible province in our capacity for action. By action here Kant means human undertakings which are guided by principles. Conduct in relation to other individuals which is governed by principles is commonly called morality. Morality Kant sees then as evidence of reason, and the ethical dimension of Christianity he sees as impressive historical proof of the existence of reason.

Practical reason and the postulate of God therefore go together with Kant. Although it is beyond our capacities to demonstrate that God exists as a being in nature, it is not beyond our capacities to show that the notion of God is essential to the practice of morality. Kant sees it as our duty to promote the highest good. For us to seek to achieve the highest good through our conduct we find it necessary to presuppose a higher being. We have a need, arising from our sense of duty, to suppose God's existence.[30]

In *Kant's Political Philosophy* I try to show how Kant's view of religion is connected to his general view of progress.[31] I suggest that for Kant there is a moral dimension to the recognition of international law and the achievement of international peace and this moral dimension is the same as the practical goal which is set for us by religion. I want to follow through this suggestion more fully here.

The problem posed to us by religion is how is it we can leave the ethical state of nature. By the ethical state of nature Kant means the normal human enviroment of competition, avarice and greed. We are continually subject to radical evil which Kant thinks is not implanted in our nature but is always a possible course for us since we are free. We can use this freedom both for good and evil. So evil for Kant is a propensity which we may potentially have under our control.

We can leave the ethical state of nature by forming a church with others. There are two kinds of church: the church visible and the church invisible. Kant does not have a very high regard for the achievements of established churches. The kind of church he favours is an invisible one which would be formed by a 'union of right-minded men'.[32] This church would be truly universal in its membership: in gaining members it would accept no distinctions of race, nationality or creed. Members of this church would come to recognize each other through their propensity to act rationally and so in a manner guided by morality. In short, they would be individuals who would be guided in their actions by Kant's own categorical imperative.

This conclusion calls to mind the views of the Italian Marxist political philosopher Antonio Gramsci. Gramsci, who undertook most of his theoretical work whilst imprisoned by the Fascists, came to the conclusion that political progress may come about through the creation of what he calls a cultural hegemony.[33] By such a cultural hegemony Gramsci has in mind a bloc of people in society with influential positions who support a political doctrine of reform. Kant's support for an invisible church of right-minded people can possibly be seen in the same light. Kant sees his members of an ethical commonwealth persuading others to take a more desirable path through both example and persuasion. Part of the role of those members of the commonwealth is also to discover other potential members. A presupposition of both Gramsci and Kant is that some people are morally better than others. This may be the case. But it may equally be the case that no individual can be sufficiently confident to set himself up as an example to the rest. Circumstances can make devils of us all. So an invisible church or a cultural hegemony might be too exclusive to carry out the task for which it is created. Here both Kant and Gramsci come to rely on an elite which comes to bear a close resemblance to the Protestant conception of the elect.

Yet Kant's view of progress is not entirely elitist nor secular. We can each contribute a great deal to the possibility of progress by seeking to do the right thing in our ordinary lives. Political leaders can contribute considerably more by wise statesmanship and by adhering to the rule that honesty is better than any policy. The statesman has to be conscious of the amoral strategies employed by others in political life. If they are lucky they can convert these Machiavellian approaches into more positive forces, but they themselves are not to adopt such strategies. But wise leadership will not by itself ensure international harmony. More is needed to pull nations, as with individuals, from the ethical state of nature. Human beings are made from too crooked a material for them to hope to attain peace wholly on their own.[34] Only by an act of divine grace for which there is no empirical evidence can we hope finally to attain eternal peace. The supposition of divine grace is not one which flows from the facts but rather one that is required as a necessity by our practical reason. The supposition of God is necessary to make sense of our moral inclinations.

This is a very powerful argument from the moral standpoint but I am not wholly convinced. Kant is not asking us to believe in God in the conventional sense, but is rather asking us to have faith in the idea of a divine being in order to underwrite moral action both in everyday life and politics. Kant's appeal to grace seems to me to flow from his reluctance to look too closely at the emotional side of the human character and the fear and contentiousness it engenders. Hobbes in his account of the state of nature prior to the creation of civil society possibly shows more courage in this respect. Kant conceives international harmony as being achieved through a gradual triumph over the darker side of human nature. Such an ultimate triumph seems implausible to me and I am not sure it is wholly desirable. There has to be scope within human life for the expression of anger, the eruption of aggression and the occasional unfairness. Without conflict life comes to a halt. I am not, though, advocating a free-for-all. Our antisocial characteristics should be channelled as much as possible into non-destructive activities. This happens in play and in games. The Protestant ethic must make room for the healthy enjoyment of natural appetites. The combative nature of individuals should be given scope in argument, debate and the occasional rough sport. American football seems to fit the bill here! Max Weber saw something of this kind occurring with business as the Protestant ethic lost its grip: 'In the field of its highest development, in the United States, the pursuit of wealth, stripped of its religious and ethical meaning, tends to become associated with purely mundane passions, which often actually give it the character of sport.'[35]

The spirit of seriousness which imbues Kant's practical philosophy can become destructive. The notion that we can never quite attain the ideal can undermine morale. Less well-motivated individuals than Kant might reason: why seek to attain the ideal at all if it cannot be reached by mere mortals? Standards of morality must be set within human reach. Puritanism (which is closely related to Kant's Pietist heritage) also embodies this too-serious spirit. In its most potent forms this serious approach has been repudiated by Protestants themselves. We live though in societies where the Protestant ethic has been absorbed and individuals have devised strategies which combine everyday piety with a spirit of fun and light-heartedness. The Protestants' extreme devotion to calling is perhaps somewhat outdated in the face of a continually developing technology which does away with one specialization after the next. It may be that people may have to have two or three vocations in a lifetime. Duty is also less clear-cut than Kant may have thought. In our internationalized society we are deeply aware of other cultures and other perspectives which throw a relativist light over our accepted notions of custom and duty. An entirely methodical ethic of life now seems possibly too inflexible to cope with the infinite variety of experience that comes our way. Everyone nowadays has his or her own version of the highest good.

CONCLUSION

What remains then of the Protestant ethic, given such systematic expression in Kant's moral philosophy? I would suggest that what remains is the conception of rational action or rationality which underlies it. We might not be certain as to what is right but we may nonetheless try to work out a consistent approach to social and political action which may have its merits. It is perhaps possible to see the work of Jurgen Habermas on communicative action in such a neo-Kantian context. The value of such a consistent approach is that it becomes apparent to others and they may respond to the invitation to rational debate. In aiming at rational action ourselves we may help bring together a community of individuals aiming at types of moral and political coherence.

Max Weber's interest in the Protestant ethic was motivated by a desire to demonstrate that Marx's materialist view of history was possibly erroneous. Weber regarded Marx's theory as over-deterministic. Marx's emphasis on the material environment in the moulding of our drives and bringing about acquisitive habits seemed to Weber to be excessive.

In looking at religious beliefs Weber felt it might be possible to discover other springs to human action which might have been instrumental in the development of capitalism. In seeing a connection between the Protestant idea of a calling, individual thrift, honesty and capitalist development Weber wanted to suggest that a more voluntarist account of the course of economic history might be open to us.

Kant's philosophical rationalization of the Protestant ethic lends strong support to Weber's thesis. Kant's contrast between the limits of theoretical reason and the possible greater efficacy of practical reason gives attention to the voluntary element in historical development. Kant sees the employment of practical reason in morality as the one possible means whereby we can give reason objective reality.

In this respect Kant's political philosophy may justifiably be seen as an attempt to give the notion of the freedom of individual opportunity its widest possible scope. This freedom of opportunity should always be exercised in a manner which is compatible with our moral obligations to ourselves and others. Kant sees it as the duty of governments to sweep away, in a peaceful and legal way, all that stands in the path of the individual's rational use of his faculties and abilities. This duty applies to all states and their rulers. Freedom, equality and independence should be open to all adult males: 'Every member of the commonwealth must be entitled to reach any rank in an estate or class which a subject can earn through his talent, his industry and good fortune.'[36] Women might justifiably complain that Kant limits the freedom of opportunity to the male section of the population. But in this respect Kant is not out of keeping with most progressive thinking in his time and a great deal of Christian thought up to the present.

Thus although we should in our moral and political action aim at a kingdom of ends this is compatible with an infinite variety of material and social achievements. An individual can 'be considered happy in any condition so long as he is aware that, if he does not reach the same level as others, the fault lies either with himself (i.e. lack of ability or serious endeavour) or with circumstances for which he cannot blame others, and not with the irresistible will of any outside party'.[37]

Kant's moral and religious views lead to a liberal style of politics wholly in tune with the Protestant ethic. Each may fulfil his or her duty entirely in their own way. However elevated or lowly one's position in society each person who acts lawfully and carries out his or her job properly may be regarded as contributing to the well-being of the whole. Where Kant possibly differs from the Protestant ethic is that he does not regard this respect for one's calling as incompatible with the pursuit of happiness. The acceptance of a moral framework for our actions does not require asceticism for Kant. Indeed for Kant it is entirely possible that the moral framework makes possible our happiness. Morality for Kant should not simply be seen as a constraint but as the rational context which provides the potential for happiness: 'No one can compel me to be happy in accordance with his conception of the welfare of others, for each may seek his happiness in whatever way he sees fit, so long as he does not infringe upon the freedom of others to pursue a similar end.'[38]

NOTES

1. 'What is Enlightenment?', in L.W. Beck, *Kant Selections*, Macmillan, New York, 1988, p42. *Akademie Ausgabe*, Berlin, 1902, VIII, p.35
2. E. Cassirer, *Kant's Life and Thought*, Yale University Press, New Haven, 1981, p.13
3. R. L. Gawthrop, *Pietism and the Making of Eighteenth Century Prussia*, Cambridge University Press, Cambridge, 1993, p.xi
4. Ibid., p.12
5. Ibid., p.xi
6. Ibid., pp.106–7
7. Ibid., p.107
8. Ibid., p.110
9. Ibid., p.111
10. Ibid., p.112
11. Ibid.
12. Ibid., p.113
13. I. Kant, *Religion within the Limits of Pure Reason Alone*, tr. T. M. Greene and H. Hoyt, Harper, New York, 1960, introduction, p.xxxii
14. I. Kant, *Critique of Practical Reason*, tr. L. W. Beck, Bobbs-Merrill, Indianapolis, 1978, p.130; *Akademie Ausgabe*, Berlin, 1902, p.125
15. I. Kant, *The Protestant Ethic and the Spirit of Capitalism*. tr. T. Parsons, Unwin, London, 1984, p.80
16. Ibid., p.81
17. Ibid., p.11
18. Ibid., p.129
19. Cf. D. Hall (ed.), *Puritanism in Seventeenth-Century Massachusetts*, Holt Rinehart and Winston, New York, 1968
20. I. Kant, *Protestant Ethic*, p.129
21. Ibid., p.131
22. Ibid., p.130
23. Ibid., p.134
24. Ibid., p.139
25. 'Pietists of the day believed that religiousness within the Christian tradition, if it is to be meaningful, must involve the complete religious renewal of the individual believer ... The fruit of such a renewal must become visible in the form of "piety", that is, a life expressive of the love for God and men and built upon a vivid sense of the reality of God's presence in all situations of life.' *The Encyclopedia of Religion*, ed. M. Eliade, Macmillan, New York, 1987, p.324
26. I. Kant, *Religion*, pp.119–20. As Allen Wood puts it, 'Kant himself was in many ways a "modernist" and even an "existential" theologian of personal commitment, a religion whose source was the "existential" predicament of finite human nature. His attitude towards churches and scriptures, as exhibited in *Religion within the Bounds of Reason Alone* and the *Contest of the Faculties*, was anything but a traditionalist one.' *Kant's Rational Theology*, Cornell University Press, 1978, p.150
27. C. Webb, *Kant's Philosophy of Religion*, Oxford, 1926, p.201
28. Ibid., p.205

29.   Ibid., p.206
30.   I. Kant, *Critique of Practical Reason*, p.130; *Akademie Ausgabe*, V, p.126
31.   H. Williams, *Kant's Political Philosophy*, Blackwell, Oxford, 1983, pp.260–1
32.   I. Kant, *Religion*, p.140
33.   A. Gramsci, *Prison Notebooks*, Lawrence & Wishart, London, 1976
34.   I. Kant, *Religion,* p.91
35.   I. Kant, *Protestant Ethic*, p.182
36.   H. Reiss, (ed.) *Kant's Political Writings* Cambridge, 1977, p.75; *Akademie Ausgabe*, p.292
37.   H. Reiss, *Kant's Political Writings*, pp.76–7; *Akademie Ausgabe*, VIII, p.293
38.   H. Reiss, *Kant's Political Writings*, p.74; *Akademie Ausgabe*, VIII, p.291

2 Nietzsche and Fascism

INTRODUCTION

Nietzsche presents an iconoclastic philosophy which goes beyond the traditional boundaries of western thought, particularly the boundaries of western thought as they have been shaped by the Christian religion. The son of a Lutheran clergyman his philosophy has the air of an individual who wishes to get away as far as possible from his own roots. Nietzsche's philosophy will forever be associated with the undermining of religious belief and the notion of the 'death of god'. In place of God Nietzsche puts the active human will which has, in his view, the capacity in the very few to shape a world of its own. Because of its identification with the decline of religious belief and any absolute presuppositions, Nietzsche's philosophy is often identified as an important starting point for postmodernism. Nietzsche's view of experience is radically centred upon the human individual. As Warren puts it, 'he reconceives central ideals of modern rationalism, especially the ideal of humans as agents with capacities for freedom, sovereignty, reciprocity and responsibility'.[1] With Nietzsche freedom, sovereignty, reciprocity and responsibility are not grounded in any metaphysical belief or in a conception of an interpersonal reason. They derive solely from the life of self-conscious, active individuals.

Not surprisingly, Nietzsche does not fall into the general pattern of political theory which is often itself a product of modern rationalism. His political theory reflects his iconoclastic philosophy in moving away from the set points of modern political thinking. The relation between the individual and the state is a central concern of modern political theory, as it has been in a great deal of earlier political thought. Nietzsche tries to transcend this approach with one which is centred upon the individual in the context of the species. Keith Ansell-Pearson pertinently notes that 'Nietzsche's thought is not that of an anti-political thinker but of someone who sets out to challenge the conception of the political found in modern thought.'[2] In contrast to traditional political theory, the state is not the centrepoint of Nietzsche's political concern. Nietzsche is concerned with the fate of the individual and, above all, the fate of the one supremely talented individual. He sees this individual in the context not of one nation, state or class but rather in a European and universal context. This broadening of the perspective of political thought to a European and world perspective may have disappointing consequences with

Nietzsche himself, in that he turns it into a profoundly egoistic doctrine, nonetheless he opens the way for a critical view of modern political thinking and ideologies.

THE ISSUE

I think I would have a great deal of support if I were to suggest that Fascism, as experienced in central and southern Europe between 1918–1945, represents a wrong turning for western civilisation. This is a view which is probably shared by all those who adhere to the humanist tradition prominent in both liberal and socialist political thought. From the standpoint of this tradition Fascism appears not only as a thoroughly distasteful doctrine, but also as one ultimately impractical within the political context. It is not clear that we can draw the same entirely derogatory conclusion about the politics which might flow from Nietzsche's social thinking – such as it is.

Nietzsche is not conspicuously a social and political thinker. His main emphasis appears to be on individual ethical action. However, a view of individual ethical activity is perforce a social outlook. Virtue primarily concerns our relationship to others as well as ourselves. The social outlook that appears to emanate from Nietzsche's philosophy is, it might fairly be said, one of cultural elitism and consequent indifference towards the masses. Nietzsche is unapologetically contemptuous of mass life. He sees the majority of people as incurably stupid and worthy only of subordination. He appears prepared, as a consequence, to divide the teaching of ethics into two. For the unintelligent majority he appears to recommend a slave morality. This is a subordinate morality, such as the doctrine of morality offered by the Christian church. And for the intelligent and dominant minority he is prepared to recommend a master morality of continual challenge and conflict. It is this master morality he is concerned to develop in his ethical thinking.

The ethic of the master morality Nietzsche has himself to create as he finds very little at hand in contemporary western culture. With his writing in general, Nietzsche appears to be able to draw some inspiration from classical literature and culture, especially the myth of Dionysius the Greek God of wine – and it may be true that his view of morality is also drawn from this source. Nietzsche admired greatly the style of life of the ancient Greek nobility and although he realized it could not be recovered in the modern era, he nonetheless thought lessons might be drawn from it. Two possible inspirations for Nietzsche's master morality in the modern era might be Machiavelli and Hobbes. With his emphasis on the *virtu* or audacity of the *Prince*, Machiavelli may have afforded inspiration for Nietzsche. Equally,

Hobbes's account of political *Leviathan* which has to dominate all aspects of domestic political life may have chimed in with Nietzsche's views of power. A view I want to suggest here is that, although the Fascist doctrine is ultimately implausible and inoperable from the standpoint of the maintenance of western culture, Nietzsche's elitist view might well turn out to be practicable. It is not one I personally like, but I can see that life might be possible if one adopted one or other of Nietzsche's ethics. Choosing to be subordinate one might, by adopting Christian maxims such as 'blessed are the meek', lead a reasonably successful or satisfactory life. If one, on the other hand, has the means and the determination, one might successfully lead a dominant life by adopting Nietzsche's (arrogant) elitism. In short, it might be thought that Nietzsche offers the individual strategies for survival in the modern world.

THE WILL TO POWER

What rings true about Nietzsche's vitalist approach – an approach shared by the theoretically-minded Fascists – is its stress upon the arbitrary nature of human experience. Life is, for Nietzsche, what seems to come first. The world is at it appears to us: a multiplicity of sensations, instincts, drives and events with no inherent order. What order exists is that given to it by the individual through his activity. Thus, Nietzsche breaks from the Enlightenment tradition in making no universalist claims about human knowledge and experience. What we feel and know is bound in with the perspective of our individual experience.[3]

This may be an unwelcome conclusion for Nietzsche to draw, but it is one which appears to tie in with the complexities of modern experience. In Nietzsche's own time greater acquaintance with non-European civilisations and the greater spatial and social mobility within Europe itself may have led to an awareness of the relative nature of social norms and values. The growth of science was extremely rapid in the latter half of the nineteenth century but this growth was not unilinear. Dispute and controversy were arguably a hallmark of the development of science. Nietzsche gave vent to the scepticism of his time in drawing his reader's attention to the partiality of knowledge and, of course, with such books as *Beyond Good and Evil* he drew particular attention to the partiality of our ethical beliefs.

Nietzsche's view appears to be that it is those who are on top in life who dictate human values. Following Thrasymachus in Plato's *Republic* Nietzsche seems to hold that 'justice is what is in the interest of the stronger party'.[4] The will to power plays an essential part in social life. What drives the individual on in life is the desire to master his situation by mastering others.[5]

Nietzsche appears not only to suggest but to welcome the fact that all social relations are tainted by power.

With Nietzsche the will to power is a never-ending and overriding principle of human experience. Although Nietzsche wishes to distance himself from traditional philosophy in not propounding that there is one rational principle which underlies the universe, he does not escape the temptation of making fundamentalist statements. But in his case the fundamentalist statement is one which is hostile to rationalism. It is also different in that it is not a reflective principle. He does not try to say what the universe is *in itself*, rather he attempts to state what the universe must be *for us*. As Warren puts its, with Nietzsche 'the concept of will to power' is 'a critical ontology of practice'.[6] Nietzsche believes he cannot in the style of traditional philosophy generalize about being as such, but he does believe that he can state with some accuracy what being is like *for us*.

It appears to me to be plausible to suggest that little is achieved in social life without power. Even the provision of the basic essentials of life requires some power over one's environment, be it only in the less immediately apparent form of the possession of money to buy the goods and services which we require. Dealing with people on a friendly and equal basis for instance, also involves some political use of power. Without the power to punish digressions from this friendliness and equality, relations may well easily break down. This kind of power we tend though to take for granted. Generally, it is embodied in habit and customary morality. In some relationships it is subordinate to other considerations such as love and respect. However, the need for it to exist does illustrate Nietzsche's point that the possibility of the exercise of power is probably necessary in order to sustain the most ordinary of human relations. 'What is good?', he says, 'all that heightens the feeling of power, the will to power, power itself in men: What is bad? – all that proceeds from weakness.'[7]

What I think follows from Nietzsche's stress on power, and his equal stress on the arbitrary aspect of knowledge and human experience, seems to be the need to put greater emphasis on the role of assertiveness in the making of our experience. Following Nietzsche's view, the assertive person will define his or her individual situation more effectively than the non-assertive. And since, to follow further Nietzsche's line of thought, the whole of our experience is built up as a result of one person or other's (or a society's) assertiveness, then in asserting ourselves we help build our common experience. The more the individual effectively says and does, the more the world may become his or her own. Nietzsche joins the modernist movement in concluding it is we that make our own world.

FASCISM AND THE ETHOS OF POWER

Getting there first, so to speak, takes on a primary significance. There is no world – no experience without someone or other asserting themselves. In any situation the first person or society to assert themselves successfully helps set the agenda. This insight – which Nietzsche shares, I think with modern political activism was one seized upon with remarkable effect by the Fascists. From the March on Rome to the final days of the Third Reich in Hitler's bunker in Berlin in 1945, the Fascists sought always to seize the initiative. They sought at all times to dominate the agenda of European political life. The liberal belief in having an open agenda for each to stamp on it his or her own character is easily swamped by those who more effectively understand the rules of the game or, rather, how to subvert the rules of the game. In social and political life the most important item does not necessarily rise to the top. Somebody has to decide priorities. The activist/Fascist knows how to establish precedence.

What I am describing here is the possible breakdown of one pattern of civilization. Historically the agenda of social life has, on the whole, been set by social tradition, custom and habit. To adopt the style of life advocated by Nietzsche for the elite, and recommended by the Fascists for society as a whole, means a continual drive towards novelty and change. This I take to be the modernist spirit. Capped by an amoral pursuit of power. Instead of accepting the rules ready to hand and trying to alter or reform them to suit one's purpose, the individual and society may write the rules as they go along. For Nietzsche elite life is characterized by the absence of fixed ethical and social rules.

There is a marked radical trend in Fascist politics.[8] Hitler and Mussolini both wanted to break decisively with the past. They disliked parliamentary democracy because thay saw it as a political system ill-designed to achieve a purpose rapidly. The Fascists shared with the futurists a love of speed, modern machinery, and clear angular designs, symbolized most dramatically by the modern aeroplane. Nietzsche did not himself live to see these dramatic developments in technology but they appear to be in keeping with the iconoclastic nature of his thinking. What, however, appears to mark off Nietzsche's iconoclasm from that of the futurists and the fascists is that it is an iconoclasm with a clear purpose. Nietzsche sought to establish a successful elite culture which sustained, as he saw them, the higher values of European civilization. Nietzsche had no direct interest in technology or gutter politics. The noble type of man feels himself to be the deliverer of values, he does not need to be approved of, he judges 'what harms me is harmful in itself'.[9] He disdained the life of the man in the street, whereas Fascists sought to give expression to their radicalism by raising the mass. Gutter politics was their true element.

Fascism was a politics of *show* . Fascists lived by and for appearances. Their adherence to modernity was in keeping with the spirit of times. Often devoid of original ideas Fascists culled from those around them, in many instances their opponents – such as the Marxists – techniques and practices which drew attention to themselves. Other than pursuing power and staying in the limelight, Fascist leaders seemed not to have a wholly clear vision of the kind of society they would wish to see. Fascists seemed often to read back from what brought success in the circus of modern life to what their purposes and values ought to be. Theirs was a truly derivative morality. In the Fascists' view of the world, morality was subordinate to power.

For those committed to the politics of appearance the contemporary era offers enormous opportunities. Above all, in the expansion of the means of communication – exemplified in the development of a national radio service and large chains of cinemas showing the latest newsreels and films – Fascists were presented on a 'stage' which was commensurate with their inflated ambitions. Hitler made a point of travelling to and from his campaign rallies by aeroplane. This enabled him to stage the most dramatic arrival and departure.

The mode of arriving and departing from such rallies was arguably as important to the overall effect as the speeches themselves. Even the speeches were primarily means for self-display. The stress was always upon the form rather than the content. Rhetoric took precedence over argument. In contrast, the realm of appearances interested Nietzsche, but only as a transition point to more substantial things – the life of the *Übermensch* (*overman*). It is to the life of the *Übermensch* we now turn.

ELITISM AS A COUNTER TO DEMOCRACY

According to Nietzsche, 'the demagogic character and the intention to influence the masses is now common to all political parties'.[10] In his view we are in a sorry state where the masses begin to reason for themselves and demand self-fulfilment. They are too ignorant for that. The only laudable aim for society is to create a higher culture, and such a higher culture can only come into being 'where there are two different castes in the society ... the caste of forced-labour and the caste of free labour'.[11] The idea that society should be governed by utilitarian principles which require the greatest happiness of the greatest number runs counter to the preservation of a higher culture. It should not, therefore, be countenanced. Instead of the minority being subordinate to the needs of the majority, the society should be organized in such a way that the majority is subordinate to the privileged minority.

Nietzsche described his utopia as being a society in which hard work and need is apportioned to those who least suffer by it,[12] and conversely where leisure and pleasure are apportioned to those who can most take advantage of them. He wishes to see prosper an aristocracy of the sensitive and the cultured. A society where the *Übermensch* is properly at home. He believes that instead of society dedicating itself to the welfare of the whole (or the masses), it should dedicate itself to the welfare of the few.

Whatever the affinities we may detect between Nietzsche's doctrines and those of Fascism, Nietzsche was seemingly not a *Nationalist*. He regarded nationalism as a morbid, pathological development. He believed that trade and industry and the general commerce among nations was slowly undoing the different national groupings of Europe. What would eventually transpire, he thought, would be a Europe made up of mixed races, and there should be no reason why the Jews should not be regarded as an essential ingredient in this mix.[13] The Germans could, with their knowledge of languages, play an important mediating role in creating a mixed European society. The intelligent person will consciously aim at this to undermine *Nationalism*.

In so doing such a person will help to foster what Nietzsche calls the 'democratic' movement in Europe. The most important attribute of this process of *democratization* is that each individual regards himself as equal with all others. What you will have is a standardization of men 'that is to say, the slow emergence of an essentially supra-national and nomadic type of man who, physiologically speaking, possesses as his typical distinction a maximum of the art power of adaption'.[14] Nietzsche sees nationalism as arising *in response* to this inexorable process. But how is it that the cultural aristocrat can make himself support this process of levelling and democratization. The reason is that 'the same novel conditions which will on average create a levelling and mediocritizing of men – a useful, industrious, highly serviceable and able herd-animal man – are adapted in the highest degree to giving rise to exceptional men of the most dangerous and enticing quality'.[15]

The weakening of national barriers caused by the democratic movement cannot possibly lead to a more democratic society. The very adaptability and serviceability of the average new European 'will lead to the production of a type prepared for *slavery*' rather than freedom. What you have essentially is 'garrulous, weak-willed and highly employable workers' who can no more do without a master than they can do without bread.[16] It is the few exceptional men who will be called upon to be their masters. Thus, for Nietzsche, 'the democratization of Europe is at the same time an involuntary arrangement for the breeding of tyrants in every sense of that word, including the most spiritual'.[17] The new Europe will need its superman to dominate the rest of the members of society. What is required is 'a new ruling caste for Europe' – herein lies the new European problem.[18]

WHY IS THE CREATION AND PRESERVATION OF AN ARISTO-CRATIC CASTE SO IMPORTANT?

Nietzsche's argument is that without outward differences among people you will not get inward differentiation of the soul. (Hitler advanced a similar argument which he tied up more explicitly with racial theory.) The noble and elevated have to be honoured as such in society for them to gain a foothold within the individual. You have to create the outward 'pathos of distance' between the ruling class and its subjects for man to aim at reaching higher, to elevate himself. The cultured individual comes into being, it has to be admitted, through domination. Historically all great cultures have been formed through the suppression of one by another. For Nietzsche it is thus sentimentality not to recognize the connection between domination and human advancement. 'Without the *pathos of distance* such as develops from the incarnate differences of classes, from the ruling caste's constant looking out and looking down, from its equally constant exercise of obedience and command, its holding down and holding at a distance, that other, more mysterious pathos could not have developed either, that longing for an ever-increasing widening of distance within the soul itself.'[19]

A genuine aristocracy will not flinch from doing what is necessary for its own existence. 'Its fundamental faith must be that society should not exist for the sake of society but only as foundation and scaffolding upon which a select species of being is able to raise itself to its higher task and in general to a higher existence.'[20] Nietzsche wants to recommend a '*master morality*' which recognizes the realities of the maintenance of an ordered society and rich culture. Not to harm others, not to exploit them and to treat them as you yourself would wish to be treated is fine amongst friends, but does not work as a social principle. Here you must recognize *the will to power*.

Clearly there is an affinity between the politics that might be derived from Nietzsche's philosophy and the politics of Fascism. Nietzsche favours elitism, he is not wholly averse to the use of cruelty as a means of achieving political ends, he is prepared to break decisively with the past and recommends an anti-Christian ethos. Those things in Nietzsche's philosophy which appear to denote the aribitrariness of civilization might be picked on by a person of a Fascist disposition. What they arguably would not pick on is Nietzsche's dislike of nationalism, his scepticism about the state, and his pan-Europeanism. Also they might not find too congenial his interest in culture, his apparent love of scholarship and his plea for the uniqueness of the individual. Although we might read authoritarian policies into Nietzsche's philosophy, he appears not to be a totalitarian. One perspective he appears to share with the liberal (with whom he is in most respect at odds) is the precedence he gives to the individual over the state.

THE FREE SPIRIT

I am not inclined to attribute blame to Nietzsche for holding some views which were later to be congenial to some Fascists. The notion that a philosopher ought to be held in high esteem because others employed similar ideas – or may have derived their ideas directly from them – seems to me somewhat displaced. It seems to presuppose, first, that philosophers may be the sole source for certain ideas – as though people could not think for themselves – and, secondly, that there are unthinking individuals who are simply the tools of the ideas of others. The existence of such mechanical relationships appears implausible to me. What is interesting to note is however, the two distinct responses to similar problems which Fascism and Nietzsche's philosophy represent. Both Nietzsche and the Fascist thinker saw European civilization at a different point of departure. Fascism sought to modernize without dramatic change in the social structure, Nietzsche took the view that something even more radical was in the offing. Civilization would self-consciously have to sacrifice the well-being of the many in order to preserve and enhance the cultured few. Nietzsche sought a species-wide solution to the problems of modernism, Fascism tried to resolve those problems in the context of the nation-state.

Nietzsche's social and political thinking seems to be influenced by his view that the ideal condition for the human being is that of the 'free spirit' bound by few social norms and expectations (the overman) and that very few individuals want to or are capable of achieving this condition. The majority, he thinks, prefer to remain 'bound' spirits, hemmed in by the cultural social norms of their time. It is interesting to compare this vision of human emancipation with that of Marx. For Marx everyone would wish to attain the condition of freedom and he tries to envisage circumstances in a communist society, where this might be possible. It might be said that on a day-to-day basis not many of the would-be subjects of Marx's emancipation would wish to be set free. Indeed, it might seem possible to accuse Marx of *arrogance* in trying to read into the minds of other people what they might mean by emancipation. Rather than follow Marx in this respect, possibly it may be more correct to suggest that each person would wish to define freedom for themselves. This is what might make Nietzsche's 'free spirit' a more attractive proposition. Each may strive to become a free spirit. Some will succeed. Many will fail. However, the vast majority are free not to make the effort. They will be, of their own volition, bound spirits.

NOTES

1. M. Warren, *Nietzsche and Political Thought,* MIT press, Cambridge, Mass., 1988 p.ix
2. K. Ansell-Pearson, *Nietzsche contra Rousseau,* Cambridge University Press, 1991, p.xii
3. A. Nehemas, *Nietzsche: Life as Literature,* Harvard University Press, 1985, p.49
4. Plato, *Republic,* Penguin, Harmondsworth, 1972 p.65
5. A. Nehemas, *Nietzsche: Life as Literature,* p.233
6. M. Warren, *Nietzsche and Political Thought,* p.114.
7. *Nietzsche Reader,* (ed. R. J. Hollingdale), Penguin, Harmondsworth, 1977, p.231
8. H. Williams, *Concepts of Ideology,* Wheatsheaf Books, Brighton, 1988, pp.61–2
9. Nietzsche, *Beyond Good and Evil,* Penguin, Harmondsworth, 1988. p.176
10. Friedrich Nietzsche, *Human, all too Human / Werke in sechs Bänden,* Vol.2, Carl Hanser Verlag, München/Wein, p.665
11. Nietzche, *Werke* 2 p.666
12. Ibid., p.676
13. Ibid., p.686; See also *Beyond Good and Evil,* pp.162–3
14. Nietzsche, *Beyond Good and Evil,* pp.153–4
15. Ibid., p.154
16. Ibid.
17. Ibid.
18. Ibid., p.164
19. Ibid., p.173
20. Ibid., p.174

3 Political Philosophy and the Philosophy of History in Hegel's Essay on the English Reform Bill

INTRODUCTION

Why might Hegel have wanted to write the essay on the English Reform Bill at all? His main interests were always philosophical. The author of such exhaustively philosophical works such as the *Phenomenology of Spirit* and the *Science of Logic* might well have thought the dispute about the undermining of certain privileges in the English House of Commons beneath his notice. There is of course Hegel's penchant for writing the occasional piece on day-to-day politics, evident as early as 1801 in his composition on the *German Consititution*, which may partially account for his interest. But these earlier political writings, motivated no doubt by a healthy interest in current affairs, are generally about Germany and events which may have affected Hegel personally quite closely.

In terms of Hegel's philosophy the engagement with the English Reform Bill is difficult to understand. Hegel gives a full account of what he thinks should be the political philosopher's attitude to current politics in the preface to the *Philosophy of Right*.[1] This attitude is seemingly not very positive. Hegel gives the very strong impression in the preface that he finds the direct involvement of philosophers in politics distasteful. This distaste makes itself apparent in his reaction to the political activity of Professor Fries of Jena. In Hegel's opinion Fries had misguidedly allowed himself to get involved in the Wartburg Festival and other student demonstrations for the widening of democracy in Germany.[2] Fries involvement in these events had wholly undesirable consequences. Hegel saw it as undermining the public credibility of philosophy and as the meddling of philosophy in an area in which it had no special competence. Hegel's view is that if philosophy has any special insight to offer into the complexities of political life this insight always arrives too late to be of any practical value. He argues that it is only retrospectively that philosophical analysis can be found. In terms of the present the philoso-

29

pher is as much in the dark as any other citizen as to the significance and outcome of events. Given these powerful reasons why Hegel might not wish to comment on events in England, how do we account for the essay which Hegel published in a serialized form in a prominent Berlin newspaper *Die Preussische Staatszeitung*? There are two possibilities which seem to occur:

1. It may be that Hegel is writing in the past mode about events that have already occurred. In which case Hegel might see himself as providing philosophical insight, but not philosophical insight that can now allow for change for the better. Thus the essay might be a retrospective philosophical work written for intellectual satisfaction.

2. The essay is not primarily in a philosophical mode. Hegel may see himself contributing as a layman to a current debate about the feasibility of reform in Britain and its impact on Prussia. If this is so, no specialist philosophical knowledge is invloved. Hegel might be taken as trying to show that he has good political insight which those with a practical political bent might wish to share. In other words, Hegel might see himself writing as a concerned layman commenting on events that are of great interest to him. If this if the mode in which the essay is written it may then involve recommendations.

I find it difficult to discern from what I know of the historical circumstances which of these two possible interpretations is correct. If we follow the evidence of the text itself then it seems that no precise situating of the essay is open to us. At the beginning of the piece Hegel modestly says this: 'the aim of this essay is to assemble here those higher aspects of the matter which have been discussed in the parliamentary debates up till now'.[3] Typically Hegel gets directly to the substance of his discussion and allows his themes to emerge as he proceeds. What he says implies that he is attempting more than a journalistic summary and that some interesting synthesis may emerge.

At this stage my hypothesis is that the essay involves a combination of the two approaches mentioned above. Hegel may well be coming at the problems of British politics as a philosopher, but also unprepared to throw off his standing as an educated layman. But this in itself is an interesting proposition. In the *Philosophy of Right* Hegel rules out the direct participation of philosophers in politics and is also in that work wary of the expression of public opinion. The standpoint of the educated laymen is likely to fall into the sphere of public opinion and the standpoint of the philosopher has seemingly nothing to offer the practising politician in the present. Hegel has then to work for the space in which his intervention is to be welcomed.

POLITICS AND PHILOSOPHY

We might begin to help him find this space if we note that in the preface to the *Philosophy of Right* Hegel is ruling out a certain kind of direct intervention in politics on the the part of philosophy. Although he may give the appearance of cutting off philosophy from contemporary political action, what he says does not imply such a global prohibition. Fries's intervention in politics was after all a pretty dramatic one. Fries joined his students on the streets and sought to give greater credibility to their cause by lending his academic weight to their case.[4] Apparently, Fries's involvement caused a greater stir in German life and did not wholly redound to his credit. Hegel in his comments on Fries was anxious that philosophy should preserve for itself a sphere independent of political life and seemed to believe that this was imperilled by the kind of responsibilities Fries undertook. The implication is that philosophers might have a quieter, more unassuming role to play in national political life.

In Fries's defence we might controversially want to say that there is a heavily biased form of intervention already present in Hegel's political philosophy. We might see this bias as one towards support for the main aspects of the existing state of affairs. In his accusations against Fries Hegel does come across as a conservative anxious to preserve existing institutions against undue pressures and threats. No doubt this would be a crude criticism of Hegel, more in the style of Fries's student supporters, but Hegel cannot wholly escape the suggestion that he is to some extent practically involved in politics like Fries, and that on the side of the established authorities.

There is a genuine dilemma here. From an onlooker's point of view Hegel seems not to have entirely escaped the influence of historical events upon his political theory. At one level it appears as though political philosophy and the philosophy of history are torn apart by Hegel. But at another level it appears they are intimately brought together. This requires explaining. The philosophy of history is a story about the past. The writing of history itself tries to confer significance upon individual events in the past. In contrast, the philosophy of history attempts to confer significance on the past as whole. Hegel has such a story, which is the story of the unfolding of spirit (*Geist*) which has its consequence the development of human freedom. Side by side with this Hegel also presents a political philosophy. Political philosophy has to do with the present and it deals with the nature of right or justice in human society. Hegel's main stress is upon the distinction between the philosophy of right and the philosophy of history. In Hegel's exposition the philosophy of history is considered only after the concept of right has been presented. The philosophy of history is seen as a higher level of philosophy which only feeds into the philosophy of right retrospectively.

Political philosophy deals with justice after it has embodied itself in a certain social form. It deals with freedom as it has appeared, and not as it may appear in the future. Hegel then denies political philosophy access to the future and, perversely, denies it access to the past since the insights afforded by the study of the past development of world history cannot be read into the present.[5]

This is the *prima facie* picture. The philosophy of history and political philosophy are kept in separate compartments. But this is the picture only from the standpoint of political philosophy. From the standpoint of the philosophy of history the situation is different. In the philosophy of history one form of appearance of right and freedom forms the basis of a higher form. The animating force of historical development is a sense of dissatisfaction with the present. From the standpoint of the philosophy of history the present is seen always as imperfect and it is the desire for perfectibility that pushes the human species forward. Because history is seen as the product of spirit, there is an inner logic to events that presses mankind forward.[6]

Philosophically dissecting the present state of affairs does then have a significance from a practical point of view. Although discerning the tendencies of the present does not provide one with a policy that can be implemented, it does allow one to note where future development might lie. Thus the essay on the English Reform Bill might be seen as an attempt to engage with English politics to see where its immanent tendencies towards improvement might lie. There is no direct attempt to recommend, yet there are practical implications since certain possible dead ends are pointed out and certain other more promising spheres of development are highlighted.

The difficulty with this, if it does properly represent Hegel's intention, is that the approach lies uneasily between that of the philosophy of history and political philosophy. Hegel is neither dealing with the debate about the Reform Bill as a past event where distinct tendencies towards the development of freedom can be pointed out nor is he dealing with the debate as evidence of the rationality of justice in England. We might escape this conclusion by regarding the essay entirely as a journalistic piece. But if we were to do so this would take from it its distinctive character as the writing of a distinguished philosopher.

Another way of considering the essay is to follow Michael Petry by regarding it as a combination of analysis and propaganda.[7] Where Hegel is criticising the British state of affairs in the essay Petry sees him as implicitly praising Prussian arrangements.[8] According to Petry, the object of Hegel's propaganda is to undermine Prussian and French liberalism. Hegel seemingly wants to defend the politics of the authorities in Prussia by showing the weakness of attempted liberal reforms in practice. Thus developments in Britain allow Hegel the opportunity to express warnings and objections. From

Petry's perspective, the objective analysis found in the essay gives Hegel a platform from which to attack a political ideology he dislikes. If we were to conclude with Petry that the essay is propagandist, then it would certainly fall outside the ambit of what Hegel regards as political philosophy in the *Philosophy of Right*.

There is a difficulty for Hegel in the relationship between philosophy and current events. The difficulty concerns the intersection between political philosophy and the philosophy of history. In the philosophy of history the role of negative forces is recognized in bringing about higher stages of cultural and political development. Many of these negative forces are extremely disruptive at the first time of their appearance, and their positive element is only gradually recognized. Napoleon (whom Hegel greatly admired) was generally regarded as a disruptive force in European politics by the established powers.[9] In his philosophy of history Hegel might do full justice to Napoleon's achievements; however, it is difficult to see how Hegel might accommodate his radical presence in his political philosophy. Hegel's great difficulty is that he can allow for the disruption of the established situation in the past but not in the present. The task of political philosophy is to portray what is rational in the present. And if there is a disruptive force of a Napoleonic kind posing problems for present stability, then it has probably to be presented as purely negative.

If we stick to the official account of the role of political philosophy as given in the *Philosophy of Right* this contradiction is unavoidable for Hegel. As a political philosopher he has to be a passive bystander in the present. Indeed, more than this, the job of the political philosopher is to defend the established authorities, in other words, to emphasize what is rational in the present. But it seems from the Reform Bill essay that Hegel's instincts tell him differently. In the essay we can see him hinting at various ways in which the insights of political philosophy can be brought to bear upon practical problems.

GIVING ADVICE

The essay on the Reform Bill is full of suggestions as to how political life in Britian might be improved. The essay also has many recommendations as to which are the most valuable institutions in Prussian and German society. These suggestions and recommendations tend on the whole to fall in with the structure of the *Philosophy of Right*. For example, the essay discusses in some detail the strengths and weaknesses of the demands of public opinion.[10] Hegel comes to similar conclusions as he does in the *Philosophy of Right*. Public opinion, he argues, plays am important role in drawing attention to issues and demonstrating a desire for citizenship in the population at large but it is not a good guide to political action. Wisdom is not to be found in the opinion of the mass. Public opinion is 'impracticable, or, if practicable, pernicious'.[11]

It is also highly unreliable. What the public wants today it might tomorrow fully repudiate. In the second place, throughout the essay Hegel refers to the importance of a properly worked out system of law. In the *Philosophy of Right* Hegel stresses the need for the intelligibility and openness of the legal system. A state which fails to make clear to its citizens what the law is and what future changes might imply is not a rational state.[12] Such a state invites ignorance and disrespect for the law. From this point of view Hegel finds British law inadequate since it relies a great deal on common law and precedent. He sums up his disdain for such a system with the term *positive law*. Positive law is law which is not based upon rational principles. Hegel acknowledges that all laws once enacted have their positive side, but he finds that in England everything rests on this established legal right. Established legal rights in the form of privileges stand in the way of badly needed improvements. The law gets in the way of its own successful operation. Hegel's, probably correct, conclusion is that England is badly in need of 'the scientific remodelling of law'.[13]

There is a great deal of gentle advice of this nature in the Reform Bill essay. This does not mean that political philosophers are recommended to action. In Hegel's view the only legitimate political actors are those in a constitutional position to wield power and act. Citizens as citizen have no right either to set the political agenda or to intervene directly to have their way. Those who do things in politics must be those who are professionally competent to act. And it is within this circle of civil servants, individuals close to the crown and the people's responsible representatives that Hegel finds himself at home. They are his audience and they are those who do act and should act according to the rational principles he presents. Since many of those individuals could not have the time and possibly the inclination to reflect on politics (especially in the comparative manner evident in the essay) in the way that Hegel does, it seems an inescapable conclusion to draw that Hegel is recommending how this political class should act.

Corresponding with this politically effective audience Hegel assumes also (and this is a more dangerous assumption) that there is a path of rationality in politics that the trained and astute observer can discern. There is an air of impatience about Hegel's criticisms of British politics that I find worrying. Although politicians are not supposed to listen directly to the voice of the philosopher, Hegel is seemingly annoyed that they are not heeding the kind of advice he might give. Hegel's impatience seems to be motivated by his undoubted insight into political affairs. In many respects Hegel *does* know what is wrong with the British political scene,[14] but he ought not to regard this as an unique or oracular insight. Hegel rightly compares the 'crass ignorance of fox-hunters and the landed gentry' to the superior knowledge gained by a 'scientific education',[15] but the implication that a scientific education would come up with the one and best possible course of action is somewhat optimistic.

Hegel attacks the ten-pound property qualification as an inadequate basis on which to judge the suitability of individuals to vote.[16] As in the *Philosophy of Right* Hegel sees representation as a difficult issue within the modern state. Such is Hegel's regard for the sound knowledge of the specialist and the benefits it can bring to government, one gains the impression that he would ideally like to reduce representation to a minimum. Hegel fears that open and very wide representation will bring into goverment unsuitable interests and poorly experienced individuals. This is a worry he has with the Reform Bill. In particular, he is concerned that the extension of the franchise will bring to parliament too many men of ideas and too few men of political wisdom. Nonetheless, Hegel swallows the objections he might have to representation and accepts it as a fundamental part of the modern state.[17]

Given that Hegel believes the spirit of the modern state requires representation, he is still left with the difficulty of who to accept and who to leave out. He cannot agree that the proposals included in the Reform Bill are the right ones. 'In fact', he says, 'the Bill is a hotch-potch of the old privileges and the general principles of the equal entitlement of all citizens to vote for those by whom they are represented.'[18] Hegel finds both extremes of this mixture unacceptable. He does not think, on the one hand, that wealth and position entitle an individual to vote, nor, on the other hand, does he think that simply everyone is entitled to vote. The voting of representatives is an extremely important function. And in this respect the unreformed English system with its rotten boroughs, bribery and uncontested seats is a farce. The entitlement to vote should be cherished and its secrecy and value strongly safeguarded.

As in the *Philosophy of Right* Hegel suggests to the political class that they should weigh very carefully who should be given the vote. It is important that all the main interests in society should be taken into account.[19] Hegel appears to favour a system of representation which would take on an organic form. This would be representation according to the various classes of civil society. Hegel would like to see representations emerge from the key social classes such as the merchants, the bankers, the manufacturers and the landowners. He cites with approval the constitutions of Sweden and Italy which display this feature.[20] As against this qualitative feature of any system of representation, which seems most important to Hegel, the quantitative issue of as to how many individuals in these social groups are entitled to vote seems to be insignificant.

But Hegel does demonstrate an antipathy to a mass entitlement to vote. He is anxious that a large extension in the number of those entitled to vote will lead to indifference about the casting of an individual vote. This would be out of keeping with the constitutional significance of voting. The citizen should take seriously his moment of participation in the affairs of the state, but if thousands enjoy the same privilege then the seriousness of the occasion is undermined. In my view, Hegel does not handle this facet of the activity of a modern state very well. It is true that universal suffrage does bring with it the possibility of mass abstentions, but this is not because voting itself is less significant. Each vote still counts and does so to each individual. It is the citizen's failure to meet his or her obligations which leads to a low level of participation. If one feels that others' right to vote diminishes the value of one's own vote, then one may just as well be prevented from voting if the franchise extends to tens or to millions of individuals. The extension of the franchise ought not to lead to indifference on the part of the individual voter since the moment of participation in the affairs of the state – which Hegel rightly cherishes – still occurs.

Hegel's desire to see the individual's rational involvement in the state has to be taken more seriously. Underlying his critique of the extension of the franchise is Hegel's wish to see voters well-educated and well-informed. Ignorant voters can be swayed by rhetoric and money. Hegel points out that the ten-pound qualification to vote can be just as easily bought as parliamentary seats in the rotten boroughs.[21] Modern elections have created a new species, the individual sovereign voter. This individual sovereign can cast his vote as he pleases, and he may choose for himself what pleases him. The individual sovereign voter is not bound to act as a responsible citizen and to vote with the public interest and his own interest at heart. Thus voters may well bestow their vote upon a candidate as a favour in return for other possible favours. The danger Hegel sees in this is that 'electors see in their right a property which accrues to the benefit of those alone who wish to be elected to parliament'.[22] Thus electors are tempted to cast a vote for the candidate who offers the best return on their property. When voting occurs solely from this perspective the duties of citizenship are all but lost sight of. Such marketing of votes makes the issues raised by both the philosophy of history and political philosophy irrelevant to the citizen. The standpoint adopted is the narrow one of immediate self-interest.

Hegel senses in the English situation an antipathy to rational forms of government. This comes out in the diminished role of the crown in the English constitution. Hegel favours an active monarch who arbitrates the various interests of civil society.[23] Hegel also thinks a good monarch can facilitate the transition from feudal social relations of modern social relations. He associates this transition with a move from positive law based upon privilege to a rational system of law based upon public debate. The monarch can stand to one side of the particular interests which involve themselves in such debates and guide reform in the right direction, but in England the power of the crown is ceremonial rather than actual. The sovereign political functions of the crown are to a large extent in the hands of the House of Commons. Hegel thinks this has had a very damaging effect upon British politics. A stronger crown, for instance, might have allowed a more effective intervention in the parlous affairs of Ireland.[24] The domination of Irish affairs by landed interests which in their turn dominated the Houses of Parliament prevented any effective reform. The crown in Britain was not a power above particular classes, because of the strength of the House of Commons it was a power dominated by particular classes. Hegel sees no chance that any of the reforms put before parliament will change this position and he greatly regrets this.

Not that the reform will leave unaffected the distribution of power in parliament. Hegel thinks that the reform is bound to affect the balance between the men of ideas (*hommes à principes*) and the men of practical wisdom (*hommes d'état*) in the House of Commons. He fears that the number of men of ideas or principle will increase at the expense of those with an intimate knowledge of the workings of the state. Men of principle can bring to government valuable insight and enthusiasm. But they are not entirely to be welcomed. Going on the recent history of France, such men of principle can bring with them instability. Their adherence to principle can encourage dissatisfaction and impatience in their supporters outside parliament. And if the reformed House of Commons accommodate those principles it may lead to the masses seeking change in less constitutional ways. Hegel closes his essay with the thought that the election of men of principle to parliament might lead not to 'reform but revolution'.[25]

Here then is the strongest advice to Hegel's readers. He warns against reforming the electoral system too radically as this may lead to a greater irresponsibility in the people and their representatives. This advice seems to come from Hegel's perspective as a philosopher. From the standpoint of his philosopher of history this apparently negative change might lead to future improvement. But Hegel cannot recommend the positive jump to the future.

HEGEL'S RECOMMENDATIONS FOR MODERN GOVERNMENT

Political philosophy seems then to play a prominent part in Hegel's essay on the Reform Bill. The structure of political activity outlined in the *Philosophy of Right* provides the basis on which English political life is evaluated. Where the Reform Bill's proposals meet with the requirements of principles set out in the *Philosophy of Right*, then Hegel approves of those changes. Where the Bill's stipulations fall short of those requirements, then the Bill is criticized. But Hegel does not go on to imply that these criticisms should immediately lead to corrective political action. Here the rather delicate relationship between politics and history comes into play. The forces that mould future philosophical development are not immediately philosophical in nature. Hegel does not expect the members of the English ruling circles to take up his suggestions. But there is an implication that something of the sort will have to be done eventually if the society is to prosper and they are to retain their power and influence. However, the way in which this necessity imposes itself upon these English ruling circles is not explored by Hegel.

Possibly Hegel's appeal to the Prussian ruling class is more direct. We can read into the essay warnings about what might occur in Prussia if certain paths are not followed. In this respect the essay might have a propagandist element. Hegel seems to imply, for instance, that it would be a mistake for Prussia to widen its franchise in the proposed English manner. On the whole, though, the extent to which Hegel regards the principles outlined in the *Philosophy of Right* as the model for modern society is played down . He seems not to want openly to suggest what his rulers should do. This falls in with the position outlined in the preface to the *Philosophy of Right*. But the claims for objectivity made on behalf of that work seem to suggest a strong commitment on Hegel's part to the principles he presents. Who, though, is to be the agent that brings about the changes Hegel thinks are necessary? Possibly Hegel leaves the major role to history itself in the vindication of his ideas.

I have suggested that the *Philosophy of Right* and the essay on the Reform Bill might be taken together as an expression of Hegel's views on politics. It seems to me that there are very few discontinuities between what Hegel says in the two writings.[26] And for those so inclined there are a number of practical implications about the politics of the day which can be drawn from a combined reading of the works. These implications might also be seen as having some relevance for today's politics.

1. The extension of the franchise is not of itself a solution to pressing political problems.

2. Representation has to be carefully thought out if it is to be legitimate and effective. Representation on the basis of geographical districts and numerical equality is not necessarily the best.

3. A power separate from the representatives with a sovereign status has to exist to make representation work. The sovereignty of parliament as experienced in the United Kingdom creates difficulties. There is the possibility of conflict between the role ministers have to play as members of the government and the role they have to play as members of parliament. Popular appeal and ministerial responsibility may become confused. The Prime Minister has, for instance, to appeal both to party and the nation.

4. Where the reresentatives have sovereign power in their hands the possibility arises that a part of civil society can prevail over the remainder. This may lead to factional goverment.

5. Just as the executive should be independent of civil society so civil society should constitute a separate sphere from government. English society is strongly praised by Hegel for the independence of its civil society. However, a consequence of this strength appears to be the weakness of central goverment.

6. The state should play an active role in dealing with social problems. For instance, Hegel thinks the English government should have intervened more effectively to deal with the problems of Ireland.

7. The obligations of citizenship are to be taken seriously. Hegel's concerns about the widening of the franchise arise from his scepticism about the intelligence and social responsibility of the man in the street. He thinks evidence of responsibility should be shown first before the full rights of citizenship are accorded.

8. The politics of one state cannot be seen in isolation from the politics of other states.

I cannot say that I agree entirely with each of Hegel's suggestions. But all are interesting. They are particularly interesting in the light of the recent transition of Eastern European countries to liberal democracy. Many have experienced difficulties in those areas about which Hegel expresses concern. The democratization of politics has seemingly not automatically led to the resolution of political problems; there have been difficulties about the systems of proportional representation adopted by these states; many of these states have struggled to produce a sovereign power which is free of the pressures of parliamentary representation; many of these states express a strong desire to create an independent civil society but are finding the process a great deal more difficult than was first envisaged. In two areas I would entirely agree with Hegel. First, the obligations of citizenship are demanding and have to be taken seriously and, secondly, no state should be seen entirely in isolation. Issues of goverment are complex and are not necessarily resolved by following one unique kind of policy. There may be many policies which have an equal chance of success. In issues of government the failure of policy is always possible. Representative democracy works best with an educated and tolerant public to support it. And it is not only the new democracies of Eastern Europe who are finding it difficult to bring into being and sustain such a well-informed and responsible citizenship.

In the nature of things it is impossible to provide a conclusive answer to the question raised at the beginning: Why did Hegel write the Reform Bill essay? At best, we can only guess at the motives of others in acting and very often we are not very clear about out own. Hegel does not state unambiguously in the essay what his motives are, but so far as it is possible to discern from his writings, he appears to want to bring to bear philosophy upon practical matters. My impression is that the essay represents not only a profound piece of political commentary but also demonstrates excellent philosophical insight. Despite his own strictures to the contrary, Hegel shows one way in which political philosophy and history might be successfully connected.

NOTES

1. Hegel, *Philosophy of Right*, tr. T. M. Knox, Oxford University Press, 1969, pp.11–13. Cf. Howard Williams, 'Politics and Philosophy in Hegel and Kant', in *Hegel's Critique of Kant*, ed. Stephen Priest, Oxford University Press, 1987, pp.195–205

2 Cf. S. Avineri, *Hegel's Theory of the Modern State*, Cambridge University Press, 1972, pp.119–21

3. The English Reform Bill in *Hegel's Political Writings*, tr. Z. A. Pelczynski, Oxford University Press, 1969, p.295

4. S. Avineri, *Hegel's Theory of the Modern State*, 1972, pp.120–2. For a different view of Fries's role in the events leading up to the Wartburg Festival see *Encyclopaedia of Philosophy*, ed. Paul Edwards, Macmillan, New York, 1967, pp.253–5

5. Cf. H. Williams, 'Political Philosophy and World History', *Bulletin of the Hegel Society of Great Britain*, Nos. 23–4, 1991, pp.51–61. See below, ch. 8

6. Hegel, *Philosophy of History*, Dover Publications, New York, 1956, p.57. Cf. H. Williams, *International Relations in Political Theory*, Open University Press, Milton Keynes, 1991, p.100

7. M. J. Petry, 'Propaganda and analysis: the background to Hegel's article on the English Reform Bill', in *The State and Civil society*, ed. Z. A. Pelczynski, Cambridge University Press, 1984, pp.137–59
8. Ibid.
9. S. Avineri, *Hegel and the Modern State*, pp.63–6
10. English Reform Bill, pp.295–6
11. Ibid. p.296
12. Hegel, *Philosophy of Right*, paragraph 215, p.138
13. English Reform Bill, p.300
14. Avineri, *Hegel's Theory of the Modern State*, p.208
15. English Reform Bill, pp.310–11
16. English Reform Bill, p.311
17. English Reform Bill, p.318
18. English Reform Bill, p.315
19. English Reform Bill, p.314
20. Ibid.
21. English Reform Bill, p.316
22. English Reform Bill, p.317
23. Cf. H. Williams and M. Levin, 'Inherited Power and Popular Representation', *Political Studies*, xxxv, no. 1, 1987, pp.103–15
24. English Reform Bill, p.308
25. English Reform Bill, p.330
26. This is contrary to the view taken by Petry in his article 'Propaganda and Analysis: Hegel on the Reform Bill', in *The State and Civil Society*, ed. Z. A. Pelczynski, Cambridge, 1984, pp.147 and 158

4 Democracy and Right in Habermas's Theory of Facticity and Value

INTRODUCTION

Habermas theorizes in the grand philosophical manner. Although himself not a Kantian, Hegelian or a Marxist he engages continuously, in the German mode, with his own philosophical tradition. For this reason his new book on the philosophy of right *Faktizität und Geltung* invites comparison with the theories of right (or justice) of Kant and Hegel.[1] This book represents a new departure for Habermas, since it is the first of his works to deal exclusively with politics. For the most part, Habermas weaves in this book between the conclusions drawn by Kant and those drawn by Hegel on the nature of right and politics, trying to build upon their insights and integrate them into his own theory. In one respect, however, Habermas differs most markedly from his two predecessors and this is in his assessment of the value of democracy in nurturing and safeguarding justice. Whereas both Kant and Hegel advance differing criticisms of the role of democracy in realizing right or justice Habermas regards radical democracy as an essential condition for the existence and flourishing of right.

In the first section of this chapter I intend to look closely at the critique of democracy proposed by Kant and Hegel in order to shed sharper light on Habermas's support for democratic institutions and practices. It will emerge both that neither Kant nor Hegel reject democracy in a global sense and that their grounds for criticizing it are not entirely baseless. Thus, as Habermas's defence of a deliberative politics and a discourse theory account of democracy are quite crucial to his new philosophy of right, he has therefore fully to take into account modern critiques of democracy such as those of Kant and Hegel.

Habermas's new theory of right cannot be divorced from the philosophical system he has eclectically built up over the last twenty years. As a former research assistant of Adorno and as professor of philosophy at Frankfurt University Habermas has sought to maintain a link with the critical theory of the Frankfurt School. But like other members of the School Habermas has become more and more distant from Marxism. With Adorno, Marcuse and Horkheimer, Habermas shares a loathing of Stalinism and has always kept a distance between himself and avowedly Marxist political movements. Hegel and Marx are taken seriously by members of the Frankfurt School but their ideas are not slavishly copied. As a counterweight to the critical perspective of Marxism Habermas has tried to develop his system from strands of contemporary social thought and philosophy, such as phenomenology, linguistic and analytical philosophy and structuralism.

Habermas is as strongly influenced by sociology as by philosophy. He has attempted to emulate Talcott Parsons in producing a general theory of social action, and Habermas's interpretive view of the social world is strongly indebted to Max Weber. Habermas takes from phenomenology the notion of a life-world, and from structuralism systems theory. But in his writings he tries to transcend all these approaches to provide a unique theory of his own. This theory he calls the theory of communicative action.

As I understand Habermas's theory he believes that community is implicit in linguistic communication. For an utterance to be received and properly comprehended there has to be a reciprocal acceptance of a grammatical structure for the language concerned. This grammar is not fixed, it changes as the society changes but it is only effectively transformed consensually. You cannot employ a language that is solely personal. To belong to this community you need as an individual to demonstrate 'communicative competence'. Where such communicative competence exists 'an ideal speech situation' has been attained in which the participants utterances are both intelligibly expressed by the speaker and easily comprehended by the intended audience. This ideal speech situation provides the grounds for Habermas's discourse ethics where moral principles are determined through many sided discussion and the gradual emergence of a consensus. These views are taken for granted in Habermas's exposition of his theory of right. They mark out Habermas from his classical predecessors in German philosophy through the open-ended picture of reason they depict. Reason arises as a discourse with others rather than representing a fixed condition of thought. As he puts it: 'Through communicative action the potential for rationality of language for functions of social integration is claimed, mobilized and set free in the course of social evolution.' (61)

DEMOCRACY CHALLENGED

Kant's attack on democracy is to be found in his essay on *Perpetual Peace* where he discusses the republican form of government most suited, in his view, to producing a pacific society and a peaceful world order.[2] A republic has two distinct characteristics. In the first place, in a republican society there is clear separation of powers between the executive and the legislature. Those who make the laws have to be different people from those who carry them out. This is a distinction to be seen very clearly, for example, in the present French system of government. When an elected member of parliament is promoted by the Prime Minister to the government the member has to give up her or his elected seat. In contrast the British system would fall down by Kantian standards in that elected members of parliament can take their place in government without difficulty – and 140 or more do so!

The second characteristic of the republican form of government is that the laws are made by the people's representatives. Kant is not entirely clear as to how these representatives are to be elected nor by whom. Ideally these representatives should be elected by independent citizens who do not depend for their livelihood upon any other individual. This automatically rules out for Kant all women and all wage earners. Their reliance upon others for status and employment makes them poor judges of political issues and insufficiently free to develop reasoned opinions of their own. Thus, in Kant's society the number of individuals eligible to vote would have been very small indeed and even in present-day society Kant's view of citizenship would restrict the number of electors quite markedly.

Kant's emphasis that the legislators should be representative also rules out a number of kinds of legislative forms and practice. The legislator should primarily be a representative of the people as opposed to being their delegate. The representative acts on behalf of the people rather than being exclusively their agent. Now a legislator who was a delegate (a form of legislation sometimes favoured by Marx) would not legislate on the basis solely of his or her own view the society's interests. Indeed her scope for independent reasoning and decision-making would be severely limited by the standpoint of the group she represented. A delegate member of a legislative assembly is only free to legislate in the manner requested of her by the group to which she belongs. In essence the group would decide the legislative course to be adopted.

This condition of Kant's not only rules out soviet-style representation, it also renders extremely questionable the kind of party representation we now have in many western societies. The idea that the political party can coerce a member or a delegate to vote in the legislative assembly along the lines recommended by the party runs contrary to Kant's view that the representative should be an independent judge of what legislation is required. The senators and representatives of the United States's Congress (although in principle members of political parties) possibly approximate more to

Kant's ideal than their British counterparts in that they may often vote according to their individual inclination and judgement on an issue.

Kant believes very strongly that the laws should be made by the people's representatives. Any form of government 'which is not representative is an anomaly, because the legislator can in one and the same person be both the legislator and executor of his own will – just as the universal in the major premiss of a syllogism cannot at the same time be the subsumption of the particular under the universal in the minor premiss'.[3] This rules out direct democracy as a form of government since it would involve the whole society both making and implementing the laws. It is the possibility of such a situation arising that makes Kant identify democracy with dictatorship. In his view, 'despotism prevails in a state if the laws are made and arbitrarily executed by one and the same power'.[4]

Kant, therefore, would exclude the mass both from directly framing a society's laws and from carrying them out. He would neither wish to take political power entirely down to the level of the individual nor would he wish to elevate individuals in groups as a whole to political authority. For Kant we have to see our participation in law-making and policy decisions as ideal rather than actual. These aims run contrary to Habermas's project. Habermas is more optimistic than Kant about a consensus emerging amongst the people about the kinds of rules and policies which are appropriate. He is also more optimistic about the level of civic responsibility individuals will show once invited to participate in political decision-making. In one area, however, Habermas's project and Kant's political philosophy are in agreement. Both stress the need for the widest possible publicity to enhance the effectiveness and justness of government.

On the whole, though, the notion of full, participatory democracy is an alien one to Kant. He sees direct, mass democracy as the antithesis of justice. Justice is the product of the implementation of practical reason and this can be attained only through the gradual reform from above of governments and states. Kant is, for the most part, embarrassed by the uneducated enthusiasm of the people from below. Part of Habermas's project, as I understand it, is to retain the rigour of Kant's practical reason whilst capitalizing on the con-stitutional commitment of the people from below. Instead of an architectonic of justice to be safeguarded by the political and thinking activity of an enlightened elite, Habermas conceives of every adult as a potential party to the ideal of justice developed in Kant's philosophy. Habermas tries to move on from Kant's notional idea of every individual being his own legislator to the everyday life realization of such an ideal. In this sense it can be said that Habermas has not quite given up the Marxian goal of the practical realiza-tion of philosophy.

Hegel's critique of democracy is, if anything, more vehement than that of Kant. The *Philosophy of Right* stands in stark opposition to the modern trends of democracy. Like Kant, Hegel derives right from the individual will but in a circular manner which brings us back to the state as its core. Hegel tries to integrate modern individuality with the majesty of the state. On the whole, however, this is a philosophical integration which leaves the empirical individual untouched. Apart from the privileged few the majority of individuals find themselves outside the processes of state activity including the activity of the determination of right and its implementation. Hegel would like to see right brought into being primarily by administrative means rather than through the mobilization of citizens.

The power structure outlined in the *Philosophy of Right* centres on the civil service and the constitutional monarch. Hegel sees the rational monarch guiding the state, with the help of a competitively recruited civil service, guiding the state through its domestic and international conflicts. This guidance also runs to the framing and enactment of laws. Hegel argues that legislative initiative should come from the Crown to modify and improve laws to keep up with the times. These laws do have to pass through an assembly of estates, but the main function of the estates is to act as a sounding board for policy and law rather than an active initiator.[5] In contrast to Kant's vision of the law being made by the people's representatives Hegel envisages representatives as 'fine tuning' law which has already been formulated by the civil service and the crown's council.

Civil servants are the central players in Hegel's account of the determination and implementation of justice. They have the specific power to overstep the division between executive and legislature which is so important to Kant. Hegel has some doubts about the term 'separation of powers' because it smacks too much of a state at war with itself.[6] Hegel would like to see the smooth bureaucratic interlinking of executive and legislature in the name of the general good which is best recognized by those who have specialized knowledge of government. Here the public sphere of discussion is severely limited, not only in the estates which are supposed to take a responsible attitude to government, but also in the realm of public opinion. Public opinion counts most, in Hegel's view, as a symbol of participation rather than as an actual realization of democratic strivings.[7] In general what constitutes public opinion cannot (as we saw in the last chapter) be trusted and cannot form a basis for establishing and maintaining justice.

If Kant's theory of right may be seen as in principle opposed to some major democratic trends, Hegel's theory of right may be seen as systematically anti-democratic. Hegel puts forward a persuasive conservative view of justice. But he, like Kant, is not anti-liberal. And in so far as the contemporary notion of democracy is impregnated by liberal ideals Kant and Hegel cannot be counted as belonging outside the democratic sphere. Both subscribe to a notion of civil society in which the individual enjoys the freedom of speech, the right to acquire property and the freedom to develop one's talents in whatever way one wishes. Although Habermas's theory of right does not fit in as a whole with Hegel's account of justice, it is nonetheless remarkable how Habermas takes over from Hegel the notion of right as a concrete universal immanent within the present social structures, rather than solely an ideal acting as a measure of existing practices.

VALUES AND FACTS

The tension between facticity and value, which gives Habermas the title of his work, can also be seen as a tension between Kant and Hegel's philosophy of right. Hegel stresses the facticity of right, in other words, he stresses its dependence upon the existing structures of society and the realized cultural forms. In an Aristotelian manner Hegel interprets society in a teleological way as already having within it a rational form. Right is then a rational form to be deduced from what already is. But with Kant, Habermas also believes that facticity is not enough. Right cannot simply be viewed positively as commands we must obey to realize our freedom. It also forms a standard at which to aim. There is always a clash between fact and value, in other words, between our moral intuition of right and the existing forms which are designed to realize it. Right is indeed immanent but also transcendent. Concrete right is always in need of amendment.

The aspect of Habermas's theory of right which takes him beyond Kant and Hegel is his insistence that right possesses an element of indeterminacy.[8] Kant believed that right could largely be deduced a priori from first principles and Hegel believed that right embodied itself in its most advanced form in the developed Protestant state. Instead of this apparent certainty and completeness in the theory of right, Habermas advances the notion of right as essentially pluralistic. It is pluralistic not only in the sense that different cultures give different weight to a number of key principles (for example, the position of common law in the United Kingdom vis-à-vis the United States) but also inherently pluralistic in the sense the nature of the law in any particular instance is always open to interpretation. Whereas when Hegel and Kant try to bring the discussion of right to a close Habermas wants always to open it up. The implementation of law always represents one possible intepretation of justice as it is legislated for and understood in a society. This is perhaps one reason why Habermas devotes so much attention to the social consensus which must

underlie law if it is to function properly. The nature of justice takes on more
the form of a debate than a settled state of affairs for Habermas. And for him
the theory of right has as one of its main aims to outline the ground rules for
this debate.

This is an extraordinary interpretation of law and justice which throws it
into the hands of the rationality of individuals and peoples. It is far away
from the empiricist interpretation of law fostered by Austin, which regards
obedience to the law primarily as a habit to be observed in established communities, and still prevalent to this day in Britain.[9] Habermas makes the nature
of justice into a creative activity which evolves a view of law appropriate
to the times and reflecting the complexity of society. Habermas places upon
ordinary citizens the threefold task of upholding the law, developing the law
and ensuring its implementation. All three roles are partially played by
Kant's independent citizen who is also the people's representative. But with
Habermas no adult member of the society can escape the responsibilty. This
represents participatory democracy of the most ambitious kind.

Habermas tries then to turn the apparent weakness of his theory of right,
its indeterminacy, into its strength. Habermas will not allow his citizens to
enjoy the simple faith in the law of the land which Hegel offers in the
Philosophy of Right. With Habermas's theory of communicative justice the
individual members of a society create justice from the bottom up. They do
so in their rational interactions with one another. A society is self-consti-
tuting for Habermas. As individuals create the space and opportunity for their
activities they must also bring into being the space and opportunity for the
activities of others. But this is not the traditional liberal vision as found, for
instance, in the political philosophy of John Locke of self-interested individuals contracting to live in peace with one another. Since Habermas has
a view of selfhood which is socially founded his notion of a self-construct-
ing society is based more on the notion of solidarity which must in the first
place underlie any emergence of individuality.

LAW AND COMMUNICATIVE DISCOURSE

Democratic participation is not, then, a coincidental by-product of Habermas's
new theory of justice: the idea is at its core. People who cannot of themselves
create a just society live not only without a developed form of law but also
without a fully developed democracy. Like liberal theory Habermas has no
magic ingredient which can bring into being a society based on justice. A
theory of justice must presuppose the conditions for its own realization. People
must already possess freedom from patriarchal, customary and state ties before

communicative justice becomes possible. But where those conditions are present the theory of justice can point out those social structures which constitute a danger to its successful implementation. Put in another way, Habermas's theory of justice presupposes a developed welfare capitalist society, but it is also an ongoing critique of that society.

The problem of justice from an internal state point of view is how to create a social consensus for the enactment and implementation of laws. If Habermas is correct and the nature of right or justice is indeterminate, the need for this consensus is even more pressing. A society has to be regulated even if there is not a hundred per cent agreement on what the regulations should be. 'With the growth and the qualitative transformation of the tasks of the state the requirement for legitimation changes; the more right is used as a means for political steering and social structuring the greater is the burden of legitimation.' (517) A universal interest has to be presupposed to carry out laws and follow through policies. Hegel's answer to this problem was to posit a universal class that would be suited by its background and objective position in society to represent the whole. In his view the society's universal interest was embodied in this class's consciousness of itself. In practice it is the civil service which dominates Hegel's *Rechtstaat* and at the same time shuts out popular democracy.

Habermas's theory of justice turns away from this conservative vision, but he cannot at the same time close out the problem altogether. A society of autonomous individuals cannot rely on providence alone to produce a universal interest. Marx wrestled with the same problem (after reading Hegel's *Philosophy of Right*) and came up with the imaginative answer that it was the new industrial proletariat which represented the universal interest. But the difficulty of identifying justice with the interests of one class is that this can provide a cover for all kinds of abuse. Individual leaders too readily identify their own interests with those of the class they represent so that any claims to universality made on behalf of the class may become bogus.[10] There is no facile answer to this difficulty along the lines that Hegel and Marx propose. No material interests in a society directly represent the universal interest. Material interests have to be shaped and fashioned to maintain and preserve justice. Habermas's answer to this dilemma is, if I am correct, the same as Kant's. We have to rely on culture, history and tradition to provide us with the material foundations for justice. There has, then, to be a continuous process of education of political will. However difficult, the aim has to be to create an ideal-speech situation within the relevant political unit. But because what culture and history provide us with is contingent there is always a tension between *facticity* and *value*. The inheritance has to be reformed and reshaped by each new generation.

I find this distinction between fact and value particularly relevant to the condition of Germany today. It is perhaps fair to say that Habermas's theory of right can best be seen as a reflection on the practices of the former West German state. Habermas would no doubt emphasize that it was a reflection on the best of its practices, and in his text he draws self-consciously from West German and United States experience. His thesis is that even in these advanced western states a vigilant democracy is required to oversee the legislation and implementation of justice. Now, in the new German context this conflict between culturally inherited practice and the values of justice must be even more marked. In so far as Habermas's theory of justice is merely idealistic and sets up standards to which a society progressively ought to conform through reunification Germany has increased its deficit of justice enormously. Some might argue that this is all to the good. What is needed in the new federal (*neue Länder*) states is a Habermasian goal of justice to aim at. But this overlooks the possibility that the deficit might be too great. The customs and practices of the previous society may well be too deeply embedded to be removed legislatively from above through a harmonization of laws in east and west. The situation might call for a less drastic approach, allowing people in the east to catch up more gradually with western standards of justice as they get more used to their newly won democracy. The danger of not adopting this more gradual approach might be that the problems of legitimacy which the former West German state suffered (along with other advanced western nations) might be excessively multiplied by the sense of illegitimacy engendered by its seemingly too swift administrative takeover of the east. Facticity and value may become so far out of line that the ideal of communicative justice may become almost irrelevant.

BETWEEN DISTRIBUTIVE AND LEGAL JUSTICE

We need now to look more closely at Habermas's model of justice before passing a final judgement on its appropriateness for concrete conditions. In outlining his model of justice it is evident that Habermas is not only trying to steer a course between classical thinkers like Kant and Hegel but is also attempting to rise to the challenge of contemporary circumstances. He is intimately aware of the conclusions of recent sociological and political research into the nature of the modern state. Not only is his own work on legitimacy a premise of the discussion but also the debates on the increasing complexity of bureaucratic and state life and the problems of 'overload' arising from it.[11] His theory of justice is then one which is self-consciously for our times. It is a theory of justice for a mass society with unavoidable centralizing tendencies. We have to attend closely to how Habermas himself describes his theory of right/justice. His theory of justice is supposed to lead us out of the cul-de-sac to which justice was led by the social, welfare state model. (493) Unlike Rawls's model of justice – which I would associate with the modern welfare state – Habermas's model has predominantly legal procedural features. Habermas is concerned to outline a view of legality which facilitates freedom rather than structures it. Rawls's theory of justice focuses on distributive problems and attempts to outline a social structure which might be implemented through law which seeks to be fair to all. But it seems that for Habermas such 'justice as fairness' has too many concrete consequences in terms of the life of the individual which might add to the centralizing power of the state.

But Habermas's model of justice is not solely juridical. He disdains the neo-liberal path which argues for a strong state with the principal or perhaps sole task of securing the implementation of laws aimed at safeguarding the individual's freedom. Habermas wants no 'return of bourgeois society' (493) where government essentially oversees the activities of a largely independent economic realm. He rejects such a return both on moral and factual grounds. His discourse ethics which emphasize the intersubjective nature of our individuality runs contrary to the view of individuality found in classical liberalism, and he argues that the era of an independent corporate sphere is long since over. Thus the state which acts solely as a nightwatchman guarding those areas where individual interests malevolently or inadvertently clash is an impossibility.

But the essential task of a theory of justice is to outline those rules which make possible and facilitate legitimate and free social interaction. Habermas agrees wholeheartedly with liberals that procedure is important. But he won't have it that the project of socialism should be abandoned. He knows that the collapse of communism in the Soviet Union and Eastern Europe has left the socialists disarmed but Habermas is not going to give up. (1992)[12] Habermas regards the democratic socialists as the undisputed, if somewhat embarrassed heirs, to the socialist tradition. It is this tradition that has now to be renewed and not abandoned.

Habermas then proposes a model of right or justice which is neither wholly determined by procedures nor by material interests. The liberal and neo-liberal models place too much emphasis on equality before the law when there are always substantial difference between individuals, and the state socialist model places too much emphasis on production and distribution of wealth without marking sufficiently formal equality and individual independence. The conflict between the two models centres on two differing views of equality. Liberals give equality too little substance and state socialists give equality too much substance.

Habermas seeks an Aristotelian golden mean between these two extremes. But it is not the golden mean that is crucial to Habermas, but rather resolving the tension between the social interest which presses towards uniformity and individual interest which induces possible mutual indifference. Habermas wants to come out on the side of social interest but without drowning out the individual interest. Habermas seems to me here to have the same problem as Mill in his *Essay on Liberty* in trying to limit the authority of society over the individual, excepting that Mill resolves the tension between individuality and community more in favour of the individual.

But how can justice or right do the job that Habermas asks of it? How does one develop a legal procedural view of justice which is also a material one or, conversely, how does one present a material view of justice which respects procedures? It is not surprising if Habermas becomes schematic in his answer to this question because it is not only a problem which affects his theory of right but it is also a pressing problem of our age. I see it as one of the central problems for political philosophy brought about by the end of the Cold War. It is the border question for political philosophy which is also the practical border issue for Germany. How does one reconcile two antithetical views of justice: the one which sees justice as the upholding of an independently determined law and the other which sees justice as a certain material distribution of resources?

I think it is very much to Habermas's credit that he sees the issue from the border. He favours neither legal proceduralism nor distributivism. The critique of capitalism has to be sustained although the crucial moral point that individual autonomy has to be given priority is conceded. Habermas accepts as a desirable 'dogma' the Kantian idea that we are only to obey those laws that we as free subjects can conceive as legislating for ourselves. (537) Capitalism is not to be done away with, but the power of the system has to be tamed. (493) Ecological and social issues have to be faced. Rules have to be devised which allow poverty to be tackled and ensure that commercial enterprises (and particularly the defence industries) are responsibly run. The rule of law has to be rigidly upheld not solely for itself but as a legitimate means for mediating our economic and social conflicts. Law should be seen as society's ongoing conversation with itself: never complete, always subject to revision and always to be respected.

RISKING DEMOCRACY: INDIVIDUALITY AND RESPONSIBILITY

What makes law into a material power with Habermas is, I think, the Kantian subsumption of right under ethics. In Habermas's syllogism of practical reason, ethics is the major premiss, law the minor premiss and the good society is the conclusion. The making of the law if it is to lead to the good society has to reflect the ethical discourse of the community. This ethical discourse has to be wholly unrestricted. Every adult member of the population is entitled and indeed encouraged to participate in the debate about the nature of justice. The law is not subject to individual morality, but the individual should be able to identify with it. This may seem like anarchy only if one overlooks the stringent conditions which Habermas sets for participating in the ethical debate. The presupposition of such a debate is that a consensus can emerge which reflects the necessity of cooperation. The socialist condition of solidarity enters not as a material criterion for the realization of justice but as its procedural precondition.

This has strange consequences for the distinction between public and private which is so crucial to liberal political philosophy. Habermas wants to transcend the division, without in a totalitarian manner annihilating it. Because he regards ethics as the basis for right, individual morality cannot be entirely cut off from the public sphere. Classical liberal thinkers, like Isaiah Berlin, would find this difficult to take. For Berlin the freedom of conscience implied not only the freedom to elect to do the right thing but also the freedom, if one so wished or dared, to do the wrong thing.[13] Habermas's discourse ethics does not offer such license or neutrality. If you choose within an intersubjectively determined ethic to do the wrong thing then you may legitimately ask for understanding but not moral approval. Private acts if they are to be considered right or just must also appeal to the public realm. There has to be continuity between the public and private in ethics if ethics is to serve as a basis for the evaluation of the rules of justice and law.

Habermas would tie in this bridging of the private and the public with the improvement of administrative processes in our increasingly corporate society. In his view administrative processes are always threatening to become autonomous because individuals falsely identify their personal (or private) ends with those of the office they represent. But if the society requires that all just or right actions be seen as a contribution to a politically autonomous shaping of basic rights, no one may morally escape the responsibility of taking into account the interest of the whole in their personal (or private) actions. Habermas refuses to accept that there is a sphere of particularity which may stand in opposition to the interests of the whole. He does not of course rule out the possibility of purely selfish actions but he does seem to suggest that such actions cannot be seen as directly moral.

Habermas sees this fusion of the private and public not only as normatively desirable but also as increasingly necessary from an empirical standpoint. In the advanced states individuals make demands upon the law which take it beyond the public sphere. Demands for affirmative action, for example, bring the law into a sphere which was previously regarded as being wholly private. The bussing of schoolchildren in the Southern states of the United States is an early example of such intervention. Following liberal principles it would seem perfectly fair that parents should send their children to schools wholly of their own choice. Equally it seems to step beyond the requirements of formal justice when an employer is required to ensure that a certain proportion of his employees is either coloured or female. It seems increasingly likely that German legislation in the next few years will have to provide some scope for affirmative action if not explicitly to help former citizens of the GDR at least to ensure that economic migrants are not discriminated against. The one movement which Habermas pinpoints as crossing the public private divide is the feminist. Here those who argue the feminist case have to be perfectly clear that they are asking the law to adjudge in areas which were formerly regarded beyond its bounds. Since the lot of women is so dependent on domestic circumstances the reform of law to aid greater equality has to bridge the public and private domains.

The classical liberal might well see all this as putting individuality and freedom under pressure. It seems that nowhere can we get beyond the law. But Habermas would answer that such a response presupposes a positivist view of law which sees law as a set of commands impervious to public debate. For the individual who feels threatened by the incursion of procedural justice into seemingly private realms Habermas recommends democratic participation. Habermas argues that autonomy cannot be realized privately. If you are to safeguard your private rights you have to practice your rights as a state citizen. (515) Rights do not exist in a vacuum, they evolve from the day-to-day mutual recognition that makes possible a civil society. It is effective and harmonious societal interaction that produces rights and not declarations of right which produce societal interaction.

This insight sheds important light on the present German situation. The simple incorporation of the eastern states in with the west does not, as everyone can now see, lead to an immediate and successful new society. There is no automatic means of transferring to the east the same levels of right and democracy as the west. The levels of right and democracy in the east were embedded in their existing practices. In many respects (particularly in the economic sphere) the standards set in these practices fell below those of the west but in many respects also these standards were simply different. In Habermas's terms the rights corresponded to different cultural forms. Unless they are handled sympathetically such cultural differences may give grounds for permanent friction. Habermas's theory of right can cope with conflicts within communities of a similar cultural type but can it cope with conflicts between communities with different cultural heritages? For Habermas progress in the continuous determination of justice depends upon a democratic consensus, but where the basis for that consensus does not exist problems arise. Following Habermas's model it seems that the German people have to strive not only for consensus but also for a common, cross-cultural and ideological perception of justice.

If we return to our theme of the role of democracy in Habermas's theory of right we can see that Habermas does not answer all the problems raised by Kant and Hegel in their criticisms of democracy. In a sense Habermas takes a great gamble with right and justice by opening them up to mass democratic determination. For all their apparent elitism, Kant and Hegel's approaches do obviate some of the influence of sheer ignorance upon the making of laws and the implementing of policy and they provide (especially Kant) a context for rational debate. In contrast Habermas's model looks something like a free-for-all. Everyone concerned has to join in the debate. No adult escapes the responsibility of being an active citizen. But does everyone want to join in and is everyone competent to do so?

On the one hand it seems as though political wisdom requires a restricted sphere of open, public debate. In such a context issues may be calmly aired and rationally deliberated by people with the time, knowledge and necessary skills. On the other hand, the actual development of modern society is very much in the direction envisaged by Habermas. People want to get involved, feel competent to get involved and, even if they belong to the diffident minority, are drawn willy-nilly into the political process. Politics has become so obligatory that we are even able to suffer from a surfeit of it. Whatever our hankerings after a restricted representative democracy the tide of events dictates a more comprehensive open debate, not only within states but also beyond their borders. But this debate is unlikely to flow in an entirely trouble free way. Discourse ethics may well set the parameters for such a debate but can society live up to this ideal? This is not only a gamble Habermas takes, it is a gamble we may all have to take.

NOTES

1. J. Habermas, *Faktizität und Geltung Beiträge zur Diskurstheorie des Rechts und des demokratischen Rechtsstaats*, Suhrkamp, Frankfurt am Main, 1992. Page numbers in parentheses in the text refer to this book.

2. *Kant's Political Writings*, tr. H. Reiss, Cambridge, 1977, p.101; *Akademie Ausgabe*, Berlin, 1902–68, VIII, p.352
3. H. Reiss, *Kant's Political Writings*, p.101; *Akademie Ausgabe*, VIII, p.352
4. H. Reiss, *Kant's Political Writings*, p.101; *Akademie Ausgabe*, VIII, p.352
5. G. W. F. Hegel, *Philosophy of Right*, tr. T. M. Knox, Oxford, 1969, paragraph 301, p.196
6. Ibid., paragraph 272, p.175
7. Ibid., paragraph 317, p.204
8. J. Habermas, *Faktizität und Geltung*, chapter 5: 'Unbestimmtheit des Rechts und Rationalitat des Rechtsprechens', pp.238–72
9. W. L. Morison, *John Austin*, Edward Arnold, London, 1982, pp.186–90
10. Cf. S. Lukes, *Marxism and Morality*, Oxford University Press, 1985, pp.146–7
11. J. Habermas, *Faktizität und Geltung*, pp.438–67
12. J. S. Mill, *On Liberty*, Oxford University Press, 1971, pp.92–3
13. I. Berlin, *Four Essays on Liberty*, Oxford University Press, 1971, p.129

5 Democracy and Human Freedom

Anyone embarking on the discussion of a topic as complex as democracy and human freedom must expect to come up with more problems than answers. In the first place the meaning of both terms is so hotly contested that it is hard to arrive at mutually agreed definitions which might allow a clear debate to proceed. Everyone has their own view of both democracy and freedom, informed, misinformed or even deformed. Quite often the possibility that an individual's conception of democracy or freedom is based upon an incomplete understanding of either or both does not prevent individuals from wishing to implement their conceptions. Often, the reverse is the case. The misinformed individual may nonetheless be determined to implement his or her incomplete view. The desire to reduce complexity may lead to the most drastic efforts at implementation! Secondly, even if some measure of agreement can be obtained about the meanings of the separate terms of democracy and freedom complete anarchy may nonetheless characterize the attempts to combine or reconcile the two.

A wise and sensible person knows that we are talking about a complex and manifold relationship when we come to discuss the connection between freedom and democracy. You might cut through the complexity in one of two ways. First, you might reduce the complexity by dangerously disregarding the wide and varied debate about the topic to be found in the two thousand years' discussion of political life and presenting your own favoured conception of the relation between the two. In this instance you would be adding to the century-long debate, probably by thinking you were concluding it! A second way you might attempt to cut through the complexity is by patiently reviewing the debate and gradually coming to your own conclusions.

The method I adopt here lies somewhat uneasily between these two approaches. This is neither a comprehensive discussion of the literature on democracy nor a full-blooded attempt to define the term afresh. My method is more sceptical and limited. I should like to emphasize above all my doubt and uncertainty about not only the definition of the two terms but also about their practical relation. But this is not a nihilistic doubt. I am not of the opinion that in social and political theory we are dealing with issues which are entirely beyond our comprehension so that any attempt to know is mistaken. Social and political theory is capable of providing illumination even if this illumination is somewhat less final than many might aspire to. My doubts

57

have more to do with the provisional nature of our knowledge. Our understanding and knowledge is in a continual process of deepening and expansion, both at a personal and social level. Thus, any conclusions we should like to draw have to be partial and subject to improvement, particularly in the complex sphere of human action. So my approach here will lead to some attempt to review the past discussion of the concepts of democracy and freedom and their relation, but it will also be guided by my own gradually emerging favourite view of democracy and freedom and their relation.

I should like first to consider and weigh up the complexity and, perhaps (if we are honest), the confusion of the topic. For those brought up in the western world in the mid-twentieth century democracy and human freedom will appear to be fairly positive terms. For younger Western Europeans and North Americans the terms trip quite lightly off my tongue, particularly when they are in dispute with parental or wider social authority. They seem part of what one might naturally desire and ask of the world. At a surface level, they are terms which seem to be entirely compatible with one another. Freedom seems to have grown up side by side with modern liberal democracy. But all is not entirely as it appears to be. Democracy and freedom are not interchangeable terms. In my view, there is no reason to expect that the development of democracy and the development of human freedom are always identical. Democracy we might see as a form of political arrangement, and freedom as a form of human existence and expression. So freedom, for instance, might include within it the possibility of democracy but democracy might not necessarily include within it the possibility of freedom. In other words, some forms of human existence and expression might be compatible with the political arrangements of democracy, others need not be. So it is possible to conceive of freedom in such a way that it may not be compatible with democracy, and equally it is possible to conceive of democracy in such a way that it may not be compatible with freedom.

DEMOCRACY QUESTIONED

For some thinkers democracy has hardly anything at all to do with freedom. In his philosophy of history Hegel very excitingly saw history as the process of the progressive development of human freedom. Human society progressed from the Asiatic model where one was free; to the Greek model where the few were free; to the Roman model where many were free; finally, to the Germanic model where all were free.[1] But none of this implied for him the widening or deepening of democracy. Freedom implied for Hegel the freedom of thought and expression and, more particularly, the 'flowering' of personality through the institution of property. Hegel does not place much stress on the individual's social and political freedom of action. The flourishing of private property led to a great expansion in the domain of personal and private freedom but this for Hegel ought not to express itself in the development of a democratic politics. For Hegel it would be impossible for us to regard ourselves as free in acting contrary to contemporary morality and law. We should not see ourselves as free if we attempt to resist our sovereign, nor are we necessarily freer if a majority of adults is able to vote. 'The idea that all individuals ought to participate in deliberations and decisions on the universal concerns of the state – on the grounds that they are all members of the state and that the concerns of the state are the concerns of everyone, so that everyone has a right to share in them with his own knowledge and volition – seeks to implant in the organism of the state a democratic element devoid of rational form, although it is only by virtue of its rational form that the state is an organism.'[2] It seems reasonable then to conclude that Hegel saw freedom and popular democracy as antithetical objectives.

I cannot say that I agree with this conclusion although I see the good sense of many of Hegel's warnings about the dangers of popular democracy. What Hegel's comments alert us to though is that you have to be clear what is meant by democracy before you enter into a discussion of this kind. Many popular definitions – not always helpful – can be found to hand. One current view which seems to have influenced the development of Eastern Europe and the former colonial territories of western powers is the notion that democracy is achieved when each adult has the right to vote. This view identifies democracy with the existence of representative political institutions where the majority holds sway. Many of the electoral systems in Eastern Europe have been based upon proportional representation, apparently with a view to making it easier for the majority of voters to have representatives of their choice.

This consideration leads to a second current view of democracy. Many individuals take the view that they live in democracy if the majority through its representatives makes the law and governs. But a possible clash develops here between these two popular views of democracy. You might be perfectly able to ensure the representatives of the majority govern without giving to every adult the right to vote. Indeed, it may well lighten the task of constructing a government made up of representatives of the majority if some troublesome minorities are prevented from voting. In this – let us hope – improbable situation government by representatives of the majority might lead to a severe curtailment of the political freedom of the minority. Equally, it might be possible to allow every adult the right to vote and still make democracy a sham by limiting the number of individuals or parties who are permitted to stand for election. Thus the two popular hallmarks of democratic rule, universal suffrage and majority government, are not *in themselves* sufficient to realize democracy.

We can complicate things further by taking a brief look at Kant's views on the subject. In discussing democracy (in his essay on perpetual peace *Zum ewigen Frieden*), in this essay Kant found it helpful to distinguish between the form of government and the form of sovereignty possessed by a state. In Kant's opinion democracy might well be a form of sovereignty but it could not possibly be a form of government. He suggested that there were only two possible forms of government and they were the republican and despotic forms. There were, in contrast, three forms of sovereignty, the autocratic, the aristocratic and the democratic.

Despotic government exists where the executive and legislature are under the command of the one person or body and where the legislature is not made up of the people's representatives. The consequence of insisting that a democratic form of sovereignty be realized as a democratic mode of government can only be, in Kant's opinion, a despotism. 'Of the three forms of the state, that of democracy is, properly speaking, necessarily a despotism, because it establishes an executive power in which "all" decide for or even against one who does not agree; that is, "all," who are not quite all, decide, and this is a contradiction of the general will with itself and with freedom.'[3] This is a quite serious accusation that Kant makes against popular democracy. Interestingly, it has critical implications for the form of government that exists at present in Britain. In the British system the majority ruling party combines the roles of executive and legislature. The party that holds an absolute majority in the British House of Commons both has the power to make the law and the power to execute it. Thus, according to Kant's view, the chances of undesirable or possibly despotic rule in Britain are high. Kant would no doubt praise the election of representatives to make the law but would find the elevation of the representatives of the majority party into the government reprehensible.

Democracy then seems to have its drawbacks as the participation of the mass in politics. It seems possible that one can oppose mass government without thinking that the mass is wholly unfit to govern. You might well believe that each individual in the mass is capable of playing a competent part in government yet you might still conclude that the mass cannot govern effectively. Kant's criticism of democracy is largely along these lines. He believes that in any state only the few can govern, some have to give the orders and the duty of the majority is to follow those orders. The majority have to reconcile themselves to this by regarding those orders as ones they have given themselves through their representatives. What Kant's objection to mass democracy should alert us to then is the possibility that, technically speaking, democracy might not be feasible. With the best will in the world it might not be possible to accommodate everyone in government.

THREE CONCEPTS OF LIBERTY

I shall return to the problems of democracy later in the chapter. I would now like to look at the equally daunting problems posed in debating the notion of freedom or liberty. Three positions strike me as interesting here. First, freedom or liberty may be seen as the absence of coercion. We are free in so far as we are not subject to constraints imposed by other persons. This position appears to correspond with the view of classical liberals like Locke, Bentham and Mill and today's neo-liberals like Hayek. Here the emphasis is put on the individual's right to pursue his or her own good in his or her own way providing this does not lead to harm to others. The second position represents a development of this standpoint and a limitation of it in that liberty is seen as acting in accordance with laws one prescribes oneself. Kant seems to epitomize this position in his account of morality. A third position suggests itself which I would associate with the socialist tradition. Here freedom is identified with socially necessary action.

These three positions are unavoidably sketchy and can blur into one another. An example of the problems they raise can be seen from the fact that the third position is as equally represented in the Hegelian tradition as in the socialist tradition. Many of the classical liberals also tend to make room in their view of freedom for the possibility of constraint socially exercised. Nonetheless I am reasonably happy that these three characterizations help spell out the problem. They represent a broadening of the categories of positive and negative freedom advanced by Isaiah Berlin in his essay 'Two Concepts of Liberty'[4] which has been much discussed in the literature on the political philosophy of freedom.[5]

I must confess that I have never found the account of freedom as the absence of external restraint entirely a convincing one. But I am equally sure this initial reaction is overdone. What in the first instance puts me off this view of freedom is that it seems in the first a very dull view. The notion of not being forced to do something unless you want to do it seems almost self-evidently acceptable, but not very exciting. This seems to me something like the child's view of freedom. Children often do not want to comply with their parents' wishes, their teacher's or the wishes of other adults. Rather than do some educative reading children may well prefer to watch television endlessly and naturally may not respond positively to having the television turned off, regarding it as a restriction of freedom. The restraint imposed by the parent in forcing another course of action may seem, temporarily at least, to be the worst form of domination. Yet the parent might legitimately see this type of compulsion as perfectly compatible with the child's freedom.

Of course, there is much more to the negative view of freedom than mere childish wilfulness. I have come to suspect my own initial low opinion of this view of freedom. There is a world of difference between the absence of restraint a child may shortsightedly wish to enjoy and the kinds of realm of personal freedom an adult may wish to have respected. The three areas in which John Stuart Mill wished to see the individual free seem to me to be incontrovertibly desirable. I agree wholeheartedly that we should be free in 'the inward domain of consciousness', in the choice of our manners, habits and dress: 'the liberty of tastes and pursuits' and that we should be free to combine with whoever we wish for 'any purpose not involving harm to others'.[6] But I equally feel that this is not quite enough.

I must admit to feeling more at home in the third sphere which Berlin describes as the sphere of positive freedom. It seems to me much more interesting to be free to do something, particularly with others. I am especially perplexed by the apparent individualism of the negative or first view of freedom. The first view seems to assume that each human being is a monad-like entity completely equipped with independently determined wants and desires. This I see at best as something as a fiction and and worst leading to possible complacency and selfishness. I tend to regard our tastes as being formed in common with others and, as a consequence, as likely to shape us as we are to shape them. Mill's view that 'the only freedom which deserves the name, is that of pursuing our own good in our own way, so long as we do not attempt to deprive others of theirs'[7] represents an excellent principle but is extraordinarily difficult to realize in practice. First we have to ensure that people are able to determine what represents their own good and, secondly, we have to ensure they have the capacity to pursue this good. These are conditions that are not always readily met in our experience.

But here again it may be that we are exaggerating the difficulties posed by the negative concept of liberty. The positive view of freedom may give rise to problems which are equally as hard to resolve. A freedom to do something with others might become too restrictive. We are not likely to be happy for evermore simply by forming our tastes in company with others and moulding our social and individual arrangements to suit these tastes. The difficulty is that it is not easy to find general purposes that are also common purposes. There are innumerable purposes that each individual might like to fulfil, like listening to music or eating mints but we are not all likely to give the same priority to the fulfilment of each purpose. Each individual brings to their view of a general purpose their own unique individual purposes. So if common purposes are pursued by a society and they are presented as representing everyone's freedom what in fact you have is one individual or one group's view of freedom being imposed upon others.

The positive and negative view of freedom, when pursued wholeheartedly, seem to me to lead back to each other. An individual enthusiastically bent on implementing his positive view of freedom, implicating all others, will inevitably produce a reaction amongst some who will stress that liberty should be the absence of restraint. And those who continually stress the absence of restraint will sooner or later stimulate the rise of individuals and groups who wish to attain some chosen end with their freedom. If the positive view of freedom seems to encourage collective nightmares, the negative view seems equally to run the risk of collective boredom and indifference.

Thus my own view of freedom tends towards being something of the golden mean between the negative and the positive view. Aristotle's common sense approach which recommends accepting the mean between the two extremes is not one that is always persuasive but here I see its virtues. You have to guard against imposing your freedom upon others but I also think it wise to have a public discussion as to what the members of a society would wish to do with their freedom. The Kantian view of freedom as obeying only those laws for which you can regard yourself as a co-legislator appeals to me since it comes nearest to this median point view of freedom. With the Kantian view it is possible to pose individual purposes and aims which, as a part of our freedom, we may wish to attain. However, the social restraint which acts upon our purposes does not intervene from outside. This is a difficulty that I have with Mill's view of freedom. The negative view asks us to take into account others after choosing our purposes. For Mill, 'the liberty of the individual must be thus far limited; he must not make himself a nuisance to other people. But if he refrains from molesting others in what concerns them, and merely acts according to his own inclination and judgement in things which concern himself, the same reasons which show that opinion should be free, prove also that he should be allowed, without molestation, to carry his opinions into practice at his own cost.'[8] With Kant the process is simultaneous. We are not initially taken to be free and then asked to consider in what respects we are legitimately to be constrained by others. Kant tries to overcome this dilemma in taking into account the legitimate demands of others in forming our purposes. This seems to me to be the essence of freedom. Freedom is a condition we must be seen as sharing in common with others. For Kant, freedom is only possible 'in so far as it can coexist with the freedom of every other in accordance with a universal law'.[9] The maxim underlying our actions may be envisaged as a universal law. No one judges for us whether or not this is the case. We have always to judge for ourselves.

As with Mill, we may be constrained by law if we get this judgement wrong. But the Kantian individual will have at least tried to put himself in the shoes of others. Thus in acting freely we have always to take into account the legitmate interests of others as well as our own legitimate interests.

I cannot claim this view of freedom as the median point between the negative and positive views of freedom is entirely Kantian in derivation. There is more to Kant's view of freedom than I am able to discuss here, and it is doubtful whether Kant would accept that the two extremes of absence of restraint and social command had anything to do with freedom at all. But it is an individualist, socially responsible view of freedom I should like to present and would like now to discover its implications for democracy.

MODELS OF DEMOCRACY

I think it is fair to say that freedom in some sense must take precedence over democracy. Independence (except for minors, criminals and the insane) must enjoy a primacy of value in moral terms. Social arrangements which rule out independence have to be rejected. This implies that views of democracy which do not accommodate the view of freedom I defend cannot be acceptable even if in many other respects those views are very persuasive.

In his stimulating book *Models of Democracy* David Held presents nine views of democracy, beginning with the classical Greek view of democracy and ending with the participatory view of democracy advocated by the current new left. Held's comprehensive survey is perhaps too detailed for our present purposes, nonetheless I think it is worth outlining his main categories before coming to a more compressed account. There seems to be a chronological and perhaps cumulative element to the discussion Held presents. It is almost as though he is suggesting there are stages of democracy which culminate in ever more refined forms. Quite rightly he ends the discussion by advocating his own view of a beneficial participatory democracy.

The models he puts forward are:

I	Classical democracy
II	Protective democracy
IIIa & IIIb	Developmental democracy
IV	Direct mass democracy
V	Competitive elitism
VI	Pluralist democracy
VII	Legal democracy
VIII	Participatory democracy
IX	Democratic autonomy[10]

Thinkers that Held associates with protective democracy are Locke, Montesquieu and Madison. And the main object of protective democracy appears to be to bring absolute government under control. Thinkers that Held associates with developmental democracy are Rousseau (IIIa) and Mill (IIIb) and self-evidently those thinkers he associates with direct mass democracy are Marx and Engels. Weber is taken as a good example of competitive elitism, and Truman and Dahl are regarded as good examples of pluralist democratic thinking (VI). Thinkers of the new right (Hayek and Nozick) and the new left (Poulantzas, Macpherson and Pateman) are regarded as responsible for the new polarization which occurs through the opposition of models VII and VIII. Finally, model IX is Held's own.

The small-scale classical democracy of the Greeks seems the most appealing of all. Where politics can be retained at the face-to-face level then it appears most just that everyone should have an equal say in making the society's rules and in running its government. I also see the case for the protective form of democracy argued for by Montesquieu, Madison and James Mill. It seems to me highly desirable that absolute authority should be checked by the power of the people. However, this conclusion we draw from protective democracy argues against the classical model because that model may well lead to the absolute government of the majority. The fifth and sixth models Held discusses appeal least since they seem not to imply democracy in any persuasive sense. Authors who praise the democractic advantages afforded by the existence of interest groups and speak of pluralism and corporate influence seem to me to be providing a quasi-democratic defence of oligarchy. Yet the Marxist attempt to institute mass democracy, though romantically appealing, does in turn run the risk of sectarian absolutism. The elitism of the new right I find regrettable and I am drawn by the arguments of the new left in so far as they are compatible with a meritocratic ethos. Advocacy of democracy does have the possible danger that we end up having the wrong people in the wrong jobs.

Fortunately we are saved from making a more complex analysis of these nine models by Held himself who in a recent article entitled 'Democracy: from City-states to a Cosmopolitan Order?'[11] reduces his own account to variants upon three models. The first of these three models is the one which rests upon active citizenship. Held sees active citizenship as an ideal set for us by classical Greek society which has grown harder to realize and perhaps more unfashionable as human society has developed. His second model is liberal representative democracy. Held sees the liberal democractic theorist both as an advocate of participatory government and a critic of its possible attainments. Liberal democrats both want to encourage popular involvement in political life and to limit its effects.

The third, Marxist, model grows out of doubts expressed about the representative system. Marx and Engels believed the people's representatives became the slaves of civil society rather than its masters. Indeed they saw the representative state as a mask for class domination. Held is struck by the participatory ideals of Marxism but does not (rightly, I think) find the political model persuasive. Marx's account of the end of the separation of powers and proletarian democracy underestimates the role of the strictly political in human life. Marx's view of politics is too much driven by his economic analysis of civil society. In terms of Marx's own model, Marxists take too literally the positioning of the political in the superstructure of society. The political realm is a decisive moment (often the most decisive moment) on its own account in social development and not just a tool of economic groupings. The tendency in Marx's writing to see politics as an appendage of other more important developments leads to a failure to comprehend the value of other, more indirect views of democracy. As Held points out, we have to ensure that institutional structures are always available within a society where differences of opinion can be hammered out. Consensuses emerge only gradually, if at all, within a society and cannot be assumed into existence with formulas such as class interest or class solidarity. We tend to find that each individual (sensibly) has his or her own interpretation of the collective good.

This brings us to Held's own (ideal) version of democracy which he somewhat modestly does not present as a separate model in his recent article. At the heart of Held's view of democracy is the principle of autonomy. In *Models of Democracy* he puts the principle in this way: 'individuals should be free and equal in the determination of the conditions of their own lives; that is, they should enjoy equal rights (and, accordingly, equal obligations) in the specification of the framework which generates and limits the opportunities available to them, so long as they do not deploy this framework to negate the rights of others'.[12]

In this model Held seeks to combine the beneficial elements of the representative, limited government view of democracy defended strongly by writers like Madison and Mill with the positive elements of the participatory view of democracy defended by the new left. So with Held the citizen should participate in politics to the point where he or she does not undermine the effectiveness of the government in carrying out its legitimately determined tasks, and to the point where influencing the nature of those tasks does not undermine the independence of others. In short, Held sees it as his purpose to restructure the participatory view of democracy, with its strong Marxist heritage, in such a way that it meets with liberal objections. This is, I think, a really worthwhile project and I can only marvel at the fact that Held formulated it in 1987, before the watershed events of 1989–90, where the problems of democracy were raised in such a remarkable way. My own preferred model of democracy would be close to Held's, requiring democratic involvement in the family, the workplace, civil society as well as in the formal political structures, but I have a number of important caveats to add.

David Held's work on democracy forms a very useful point of reference for this discussion not only because of his comprehensive treatment of the possible models of democracy but also because of his awareness of the fact that the problem of democracy goes far wider than the state. The traditional discussion of democracy focuses on the question of the best form of constitution for the individual state. This one state is taken in isolation from other states. This may have presented a suitable method for discussing democracy in the eighteenth century when nation-states were beginning to dominate the world politically, but in today's diverse and complex international order the focus on the isolated state now seems inappropriate. At one time it may have made sense to try to construct the best form of political system in isolation from other political communities but nowadays other political entities and economic and social regimes intrude in a fundamental way into the national life of states. In Held's words, 'as substantial areas of human activity are progressively organized on a global level, the fate of democracy, and of the independent democratic nation-state in particular, is fraught with difficulty'.[13]

This conclusion leads Held to engage in a more ambitious project. Held believes that we have to evaluate models of democracy in a new context. For democracy to work, 'the meaning and place of democratic politics, and of the contending models of democracy have to be rethought in relation to a series of overlapping local, regional, and global processes and structures'.[14] Held's answer to the dilemmas of our new international situation is to introduce what he describes as 'cosmopolitan democracy'. This involves extending Held's preferred model of democracy, requiring autonomy and representative institutions, onto a global level. An example of what Held has in mind is his proposal for regional assemblies, in line with the European parliament, in Africa and Latin America. He also speaks of the possibility of an alternative assembly on a world level to the United Nations. This would form a kind of second chamber in relation to the 'first chamber' of the current General Assembly.[15] These are imaginative proposals which serve to highlight the gap between present aspirations for democracy and the means at present available for realizing those aspirations. Held's programme appears visionary because societies have yet properly to come to terms with the requirements placed upon them by the need for democracy.

A DEMOCRACY COMPATIBLE WITH LIBERTY?

I should like, however, to conclude this essay in a cautionary frame of mind. I am inclined to think that there are several intractable difficulties that have to be faced in the implementation of widespread democracy in a complex modern society. No grand synthesis between the protective and participatory views of democracy – however much we may seek it – may be available. If we consider the nine models presented by Held all exhibit the tension which occurs between the drive for popular control and the desire for effective government. Democracy implies equality and we may not all be a equal in every respect. There may be respects in which equality and liberty conflict. The great political philosophers of the ancient world, Plato and Aristotle, almost despaired of democracy as a political form. Both saw it as a system liable to end in corruption or, even worse, tyranny. Plato's vision of a utopian political arrangement in the *Republic* was aimed at overcoming the influence upon government of the confused and ignorant ordinary person. Plato was conscious that wide participation in government does not of itself ensure the best outcomes. Aristotle counselled a mixed form of government which avoided the dangers of mass rule and autocracy.[16] We cannot lightly dismiss their warnings since they both had intimate knowledge of a more direct kind of democracy than we ever likely now to experience. But we cannot proceed by their authority alone in deciding our views because there are also other well known names in the history of political thought who take a more positive view of democracy than the classics.

Indeed, the experience of those writers who advocated what Held calls protective and developmental democracy seems to suggest that a healthy social and political system cannot proceed without a proper element of democracy. But modern accounts of democracy rapidly run into the unavoidable conflict between popular control and political effectiveness. As the population at large is invited into government the more the government's freedom of action is restricted. Some of this restriction may be more than justified, particularly where it undermines the authority of unelected and irresponsible minorities. However, governments have to enforce laws and produce elements of a public policy. Laws and public policy can be rendered very confused by the immediate and direct participation of the many in decision-making. At times one may well prefer plurality in policy-making and fluidity in the determination of laws, but pressed to their extreme plurality and fluidity can lead to a sense of drift and loss of control. And the consequent loss of governmental authority can endanger freedom, since freedom requires an authority to enforce our socially agreed rules.

Whatever one's sympathies with the participatory form of democracy and the exciting ideal of playing the fullest part possible in the organization of one's own society it seems to me that it is best not to lose sight of the value of the core aspects of human freedom. It may appear that enthusiastic involvement in political life may safeguard, rather than endanger, the exercise of our freedom. But politics is about the realization of general goals and that is general goals which may not be everyone's goals. In the wholly political animal the social side may take over from the individual side. The desire for uniformity may triumph over the individual's right not to conform. Thus, if I am asked on which side of the fence I sit I have to say that Mill's three areas of negative freedom – conscience, manner and combination – have to come first. I should like then any participatory democracy of which I am part to respect my right to refuse, and to refuse to undertake those actions which may (even overwhelmingly) be in the common good. But this order of priorities does not rule out a democratic political structure. What it requires is that common goals should be consensually sought and sympathetically pursued. The achievement of a common goal might well be facilitated by the refusal of some to participate. The lack of involvement of some seems to me a precondition for the critical assessment of an activity. Converts do not necessarily make the most perceptive judges of an activity.

Thus, I would argue that a view of democracy which is compatible with the socially aware view of freedom I propose should lead to a firm legal political framework which encourages dissent but not disobedience. This political framework would exist in a society which encourages majority government but only where that majority government has to demonstrate that its policies are in everyone's interests. I think Kant's strictures about the threat posed to the separation of powers by democracy should be heeded. Those who represent the majority in the legislature should be kept distinct from those who exercise power on behalf of the majority in the executive. A democracy which leads to too great a concentration of power undermines itself.

NOTES

1.   H. Williams, *International Relations in Political Theory*, Open University Press, Milton Keynes, 1991, p.94
2.   G. W. F. Hegel, *Philosophy of Right*, (tr. T. M. Knox), Oxford University Press, Oxford, 1970, paragraph 308, p.200. Quotation is taken from *Elements of the Philosophy of Right* (tr. H. B. Nisbet), Cambridge University Press, Cambridge, 1991, p.347

3.   I. Kant, *Perpetual Peace*, in *Kant Selections*, ed. L. W. Beck, London/New York, 1988, p.435. *Akademie Ausgabe*, VII, p.352
4.   I. Berlin, *Four Essays on Liberty*, Oxford University Press, Oxford, 1975, pp.122–35
5.   N. Barry, *An Introduction to Modern Political Theory*, Macmillan, London, 1989, pp.202–9
6.   J. S. Mill, *On Liberty*, Oxford University Press, Oxford, 1971, p.18
7.   Ibid.
8.   Ibid., pp.69–70
9.   I. Kant, *Metaphysics of Morals*, tr. M. Gregor, Cambridge University Press, 1992, pp.69–70. *Akademie Ausgabe*, VI, p.238
10. D. Held, *Models of Democracy,* Polity Press, Oxford, 1987, pp.vii–ix
11. D. Held, 'From City-states to a Cosmopolitan Order', in *Prospects for Democracy*, ed. D. Held, Oxford, 1992
12. D. Held, *Models of Democracy*, p.271
13. D. Held, 'From City-states to a Cosmopolitan Order', p.31
14. Ibid., p.32
15. Ibid., p.34
16. Aristotle, *Politics* (tr. T. A. Sinclair), Penguin, Harmondsworth, pp.171–4

Part II
Problems of International Political Theory

6 Grotius as an International Political Theorist

The usual difficulty in considering a classical political thinker from the standpoint of international relations is that the international is often infrequently referred to in the thinker's work. With some political theorists, such as Plato and Aristotle, the international is only alluded to in passing. As a consequence there may not be a great deal at all for the present-day commentator to work upon and a position on world politics has to be constituted on the basis of the author's known views on politics and social relations in general. This difficulty with Grotius is, however, neatly reversed. With Grotius the problem is precisely the opposite since he directed his main work on politics to the problems of war and peace. His *De Jure Belli ac Pacis* represents one of the first attempts in the modern era to put forward a theory of international law. In considering Grotius's views on international relations we are, therefore, confronted with the unusual problem of reducing his vast corpus to manageable proportions.

In the light of Grotius's great concentration on international issues it is interesting to observe how writers in the tradition of political theory and the history of political thought have sought to deal with him. Some political theorists have tried to reduce and confine thinking to the usual perspectives of the national state. Richard Cox in Leo Strauss and Joseph Cropsey's edited collection on the *History of Political Philosophy* says of Grotius, 'although it is true that Grotius focuses upon the law of war and peace, he constantly places that particular branch of jurisprudence within the framework of a general juristic analysis of law and goverment'.[1] Thus, although Grotius's preferred perspective is that of international relations Cox believes we can learn a great deal about the usual domestic preoccupations of political theory from this wider perspective. Grotius looks at the municipal or national scene from a universal perspective and draws conclusions about that scene from an international standpoint.

Grotius (christened by his parents Hugo de Groot) led a full and interesting life. At times his life was crowded with incident and interest when he was at the centre of political affairs in the Netherlands and subsequently in Paris. At other times when he was down on his fortune his life became distinctly dangerous and unpleasant. Hugo Grotius was born in Delft, Holland in April 1583. He came from a rich and well-established background. His father and his grandfather both played an important part in the civil life of Delft. Grotius's father was to be burgomaster of the city for three periods in succession.[2]

Hugo Grotius became a student at the University of Leyden at the very tender age of eleven. He was an outstanding scholar. He came from an educated background and took enthusiastically to university life. Latin was the language of educational instruction at Leyden and a symptom of Hugo's attachment to the European language of culture was his assumption of the Latin surname of Grotius. Grotius was to compose all his main writings in Latin. Grotius also experienced political life at a very young age, being chosen in 1598 at the age of 15 to accompany a diplomatic mission from the Netherlands to the court of Henry IV of France.[3]

Grotius first chose to pursue a career in law. He rapidly gained a name for himself and in 1607 he was appointed to the high office of advocate fiscal in Holland. His position was roughly equivalent in the present day to that of a prominent government Treasury official. In 1612 he was appointed pensionary of Rotterdam where he was in effect a chief executive of the city.[4] In this position he played a prominent part in Dutch politics becoming fatefully involved in the Remonstrance crisis. Grotius was associated with the cause of Oldenbarneveldt who was to be the loser in a conflict with the orthodox Calvinists and their supporter Prince Maurice of the House of Orange. Maurice's triumph in this conflict led to the imprisonment of Grotius. Oldenbarneveldt was executed for the part he played in the crisis in 1617. Grotius was fortunate enough to escape his confinement after three years. He fled to Paris, where he was later to become Swedish ambassador to the French Court. There seems to be widespread agreement that Grotius was a much greater success as a scholar and theorist than he was as a politician and diplomat. Probably, however, both pursuits were with him essential to one another and it is difficult to discern if he would have been a better scholar or a better politician had he devoted himself exclusively to either. Grotius owes a great deal of his standing in international relations thought to the work of Hedley Bull. Bull, an Oxford Professor of International Relations, connected his own approach to international relations, which he presented in *The Anarchical Society* (1977) with Grotius's political philosophy. Bull belongs to the 'international society' school of thinkers on international relations who believe that relations amongst states, although marred from time to time by conflict and violence, possess a kind of normality with a potential for peace as well as war.

'Within international society', as Bull puts it, 'order is the consequence not merely of contingent facts' 'but of a sense of common interest in the elementary goals of social life; rules prescribing behaviour that sustain these goals; and institutions that help to make these rules effective.'[5] Bull resists the idea that the relations among states are merely natural relations in which war is the norm and peace is the exception. Instead Hedley Bull argues for a conception of international relations which rests upon a notion of a common interest. In Bull's view relations among states would not be possible where the leaders of states were not prepared to accept a certain minimum of rules. Bull's thesis is that an anarchical society, such as that created by modern relations among states, is not necessarily a chaotic or lawless society. Underlying world politics there is, as he puts it, 'an idea of international society' which 'identifies states as members of this society and the units competent to carry out political tasks within it'.[6]

In taking this view Bull draws inspiration from Hugo Grotius. As Bull says in his essay 'The importance of Grotius in the study of international relations': 'the importance of Grotius lies in the part he played in establishing the idea of international society – an idea which provides one of the several paradigms in terms of which we have thought about international relations in modern times, and that, for better or worse, provides the constitutional principle in terms of which international relations today are in fact conducted'.[7]

In the essay Bull presents himself as a defender of Grotius. As Bull sees it, 'the work of Grotius is one of the great landmarks in modern thinking about international relations'.[8] Bull defends Grotius against claims that Grotius was a mere opportunist, an uncritical upholder of monarchical authority and a callous opponent of popular resistance to tyrannical governments. Bull will not readily accept that Grotius was simply an apologist for the status quo in European life. In this respect it is possible to support Bull, since the main theme of Grotius's work *De Jure Belli ac Pacis* is a criticism of prevailing cynical views of power relations amongst individuals and states. This cynical view is for Grotius embodied in the ideas of Carneades, the leader of the sceptics in the ancient Academy. According to Buckle, 'Grotius's choice of Carneades as the paradigm of the sceptic depends on two famous orations made by Carneades in Rome: in the first, praising justice, showing its foundations in natural law; in the second praising injustice, while reducing injustice to mere expediency.'[9]

It is interesting to note that the issues which dominate the discussion by political theorists and historians of political thought of Grotius's work are markedly different from those which concern Bull. Predominantly political theorists try to press Grotius's ideas into the domestic context. Oddly, Grotius's ideas are viewed from within the standpoint of the sovereign state. This represents a strange distortion of Grotius's work, focused as it is upon the conditions for international order. But it is not a distortion which is entirely without justification, because Grotius, in considering international order, also necessarily takes in questions of domestic order. Grotius also composed some reflections on domestic political order early in his career which can be drawn on to establish his views in this context.

Knud Haakonssen in a survey of Grotius's thinking entitled 'Hugo Grotius and the History of Political Thought' takes three main topics:

1. Rights and their relationship to natural law
2. The grounds for obligation to natural law
3. The scope and composition of natural law.[10]

What possibly is remarkable is that none of these topics lead Haakonssen to consider the role of the international in Grotius's thinking. Haakonssen's focus is upon the relationship between the individual and law and the individual and the state. Haakonssen bypasses Grotius's schema where natural law is a foundation for international law and thereby also for municipal law in order to present Grotius's natural law theory directly as a theory of the state. As Haakonssen sees it the highlights of Grotius's political theory are that 'Grotius operated with the idea that nature had made possible an ideal order in the moral world, and that the function of law was to maintain rather than create it',[11] and that 'Grotius is famous, or notorious, for being one of the pioneers of the contractual theory of absolute sovereignty.'[12] From this point of view Grotius might presumably be viewed as an immediate precursor of Hobbes. Haakonssen, like most political theorists, is preoccupied with the implications of Grotius's theory for the domestic situation where concepts like the social contract, property and absolutism play a decisive role. The picture of international coexistence which Grotius presents falls into the background and the issue of Grotius's domestic affiliations is emphasized. Haakonssen concludes, for instance, that 'we may still want to call Grotius an absolutist in the common meaning of the word' but there are 'a number of liberal possibilities' in his theory.[13]

The discussions of Richard Tuck and Stephen Buckle are in a similar vein. The scholarship is excellent but the focus is upon the traditional problems of domestic political theory. In their books dealing with, respectively, natural rights theories and natural law and the theory of property they stress such issues as property; resistance; sovereignty; the foundations of natural law; and sociability. Buckle agrees with Haakonssen's view that Grotius cannot in every respect be counted as an absolutist thinker. He argues that on the issues of property and resistance Grotius was an anti-absolutist. Why? As Buckle puts it, Grotius's 'theory of property is part of a political theory of a fundamentally anti-absolutist stamp'.[14] For Buckle there are two main aspects to Grotius's natural law method:

a. a priori deduction
b. a posteriori induction based on a notion of a common sense of mankind.[15]

The first aspect of Grotius's method depends upon the assumption that the world or creation is implicitly rational. As an unquestioning Christian Grotius believed that God had made the world in his image, therefore we must assume that the world is constructed in a rational way. But natural law would apply, even if (which for Grotius is utterly unlikely) God did not exist. The second aspect of Grotius's method depends upon a meticulous investigation of the habits, opinions and customs of civilized nations. Historical scholarship therefore plays an important part in Grotius's natural law approach. Grotius wanted to demonstrate that natural laws were no more than the rules already adopted in human society. For Buckle, it is this second aspect of Grotius's method 'which most distinguished Grotius's approach'.[16]

ON THE LAW OF WAR AND PEACE

Grotius published *De Jure Belli ac Pacis Libri Tres* (*On the Law of War and Peace*) in March 1625. It is generally acknowledged to be his main work and, by enthusiasts, as a masterpiece. The most striking feature of this book from our viewpoint is that it is pitched immediately at the level of the international. Grotius announces that his book is about law and politics, but it concerns the two topics in the widest possible context. He intends to look closely at most of the main problems that have concerned political philosophers such as natural law; justice; property; sovereignty; resistance; and punishment, beginning however at the universal level and coming down to the level of the state.

Grotius dedicates his book to Louis XIII, King of France and Navarre.[17] His dedication is reminiscent of Machiavelli's dedication of the *Prince* to Lorenzo de Medici, if somewhat less self-seeking. Grotius seems not expressly to be looking for a post at the King's court, but he does praise strongly the King's manner of ruling. Grotius sees Louis XIII's political policies as directly related to the theme of *De Jure Belli ac Pacis Libri Tres*. Grotius regards the King as possessing a kingdom greater than his own territory 'in that you do not covet kingdoms belonging to others. It is worthy of your devotion to duty, worthy of your exalted estate, not to attempt to despoil any one of his rights by force of arms, not to disturb ancient boundaries; but it was to continue to work for peace, and not to commence war save with the desire to end it at the earliest possible moment.'[18] The reason the King of France has gained a wider kingdom than his own is that his policies are dictated by justice and not solely by advantage. Grotius also has a personal reason to be thankful to Louis and to praise his justice because Grotius was offered asylum in France by Louis when he 'had been badly treated in my native country'.[19] Grotius rests his hopes of a better future upon Louis, believing Louis can help extinguish warfare and heal the breaches between the various Christian churches. Grotius also expresses the wish that Louis's statesmanship can provide the link between his own scholarship and a better future: 'Hence it will come to pass that the rules which we now seek to draw from books will in the future be drawn from your acts as from a complete and perfect exemplification.'[20] The implication of this is that *On the Law of War and Peace* is concerned with political practice, but more with the practice of rulers than the ruled.

As I have said, this political practice is firmly set at the international and not solely at the national level. At the opening of the book Grotius remarks that the municipal or domestic law of states, particularly of Rome, has been extensively dealt with in commentaries. However, that body of law 'which is concerned with the mutual relations among states or rulers of states, whether derived from nature, or established by divine ordinances, or having its origin in custom and tacit agreement, few have touched upon'.[21] He means to remedy this. Grotius sees it as an urgent task from the viewpoint of the 'welfare of mankind'.[22] International law has to be rescued from the contempt it is held in by many, from those who regard it simply as an 'empty name'.[23]

Grotius's concern about international order and the absence of peace is genuine and profound. He feels he has been driven to write his work by the condition of things: 'Throughout the Christian world I observed a lack of restraint in relation to war, such as even barbarous nations should be ashamed of; I observed that men rush to arms for slight causes, or no cause at all, and that when arms have once been taken up there is no longer any respect for law, divine or human; it is as if, in accordance with a general decree, frenzy had openly been let loose for the committing of all crimes.'[24] Grotius rejects the remedy recommended by some Christian writers of pacifism or 'forbidding all use of arms' as too extreme but he agrees that something needs to be done to reduce the incidence of war.[25] In Grotius's view, there has to be a median point between allowing no use of arms and allowing all use of arms. Arms may legitimately be used in self-defence but their use in this capacity cannot be taken to imply that they can be used in all situations, so that we threaten the lives of those who are innocent or endanger the property that individuals have legitimately acquired.

To clear the way for his study of the law of nations Grotius believes he has to establish that justice is not solely based upon expediency. We do not regard as just rules that are constructed solely from the standpoint of convenience. The rules of law have indeed to be regarded as effective to count as law but they have also to be accepted as legitimate. As Grotius sees it, laws cannot be founded solely upon arbitrary power. He therefore rejects the view put forward by Thrasymachus in Plato's *Republic* that justice is the interest of the stronger party.[26] Grotius accepts that you quite often require a strong power to implement justice, but it is not that power which of itself creates justice.

In Grotius's view, there is a source of justice which goes beyond mere expediency. In arguing this Grotius puts forward a view of the human individual which is quite compelling. Grotius argues that humans are not wholly self-interested beings. They are of their nature also social beings. Grotius would not be able to accept Hobbes's account of the human individual as primarily a calculating egoist. As Grotius puts it, 'man is, to be sure, an animal, but an animal of a superior kind, much farther removed from all other animals than the different kinds of animals are from one another; evidence on this point may be found in the many traits peculiar to the human species. But among the traits characteristic of man is an impelling desire for society, that is, for the social life – not of any and every sort, but peaceful, and organized according to the measure of his intelligence, with those who are of his own kind; this social trend the Stoics called "sociableness".'[27]

Grotius sees our sociableness as evident in our capacity to speak and use reason. We like to follow rules in our behaviour with our kind and we are uniquely able to do so because of our ability to think logically and remember similar incidents. In Habermas's terms, we demonstrate communicative competence. The advantage in adhering to rules is that it enhances our sociability and encourages the sociability of others. Naturally those individuals who follow only expedient courses of action lessen their sociability and are much less accessible to their fellow humans.

NATURAL LAW

Grotius believes that all human actions are circumscribed by social rules. Many of these rules are in force even in the absence of powerful body to implement them. Such rules are in accordance with what Grotius calls natural law. Natural law is a crucial feature of human society for Grotius. The presence of natural law is what raises all forms of human society above animal life. This natural law need not necessarily be adhered to by all individuals but it cannot be rejected.

Like many natural law theorists Grotius argues for the presence of law even in the absence of a formal legal system. Natural law can be thought to govern our relations both within and outside a system of public legal justice as enforced by the modern state. Natural law may be taken to affect our relations within a system of enforceable justice because, even within such a system not every action or set of circumstances can be brought under statute law (law made by the public authorities), for example, intimate relations within a family. Family relations, although outside the scope of statute law in some of their particulars, are claimed by natural law theorists to be nonetheless subject to law. Another main sphere for the suggested application of natural law is the sphere of relations beyond the boundaries of states. On the high seas, for example, where the laws of one or other national state are no longer in force, we cannot consider ourselves to be beyond all law. On the high seas, even in the absence of an agreement under international law, we may still be regarded as subject to natural law.

In Grotius's time it is probably true to say that there was a great deal less statute law in existence than there is now. Positive legislation and the enforcement of law has increased remarkably worldwide with the spread of the modern state and its corresponding institutions. The territories of the globe which were properly settled with a recognized form of government were far fewer in the seventeenth century. In Grotius's universe where the application and effectiveness of positive law was considerably smaller than today natural law assumed a far greater importance. Natural law was possibly particularly important for those who wished to engage in cooperative and peaceful relations with individuals in other states or individuals who lived in territories outside the recognized state system. Anyone wishing to bring more security and certainty into their lives and their dealings beyond the boundaries of their state (and to an extent within them) might find in natural law a source of reassurance and a basis for conducting civil relations.

Nowadays those of us of a European or North American descent might regard more certainty and security attaching to the statute laws and precedent of the states to which we belong than that offered by natural law or an international law extending beyond the boundaries of our communities. However, it is important to bear in mind that Grotius lived in a period in which the sovereign territorial states of the contemporary world were just beginning to establish themselves. Grotius was possibly as familiar with a notion of law which extended beyond the boundaries of states as he was with the notion of domestic or municipal law. The societies which formed the precursors of the modern European states shared a common origin in the medieval Christendom of Europe. Within medieval Christendom certain customs and laws were commonly recognized which were implemented by the various authorities within Europe. This was perhaps in part an inheritance from the earlier period of the Roman Empire where a law common to a great deal of Europe was implemented through an imperial force. Thus a law of nature (from which one might deduce aspects of a law of nations) would maybe seem less at odds with the existence and implementation of various types of municipal law than it does now.

This point is put well by John Figgis in a study we shall return to later. In Figgis's view, in the European context civil or municipal law (based on the Roman model) had developed alongside a wider conception of law. The strengths and weaknesses of the civil law system of Rome were themselves largely responsible for this process. 'Had the Civil Law stood alone', he says, 'its system was too hard and sometimes too narrow for a code of international morality to have been founded on it; nor did it, except here and there, contemplate international relations. But it did not stand alone. For centuries men had been expounding it side by side with another system believed to be of equal or higher authority, and that system led on to the introduction of principles from any other sources.' Roman civil law provided a foundation, 'it was everywhere, France, Scotland, Spain, half accepted, i.e., its principles were generally regarded as decisive. They could be employed when nothing prevented it. Very often feudal rights and private privilege or local custom or national habit did prevent it. In this way men were familiarised with a notion of a law universal in scope, commanding general reverence and awe, but yet not everywhere and always decisive like a modern statute or the Code Napolean.'[28]

Grotius has no difficulty with the juxtaposition of natural and municipal law. In his view both forms of law have a common origin. As Grotius sees it, municipal law has its origin in natural law. He puts this point in a very interesting way: 'Again, since it is a rule of the law of nature to abide by pacts (for it was necessary that among men there be some method of obligating themselves one to another, and no other natural method can be imagined), out of this source the bodies of municipal law have arisen.'[29] The success of the idea of social contract within a state depends on a preparedness to abide by contract in the first instance. The multiplicity of laws of a civil state cannot be enforced in all their detail continuously by the power of the state. Without some form of consent any positive legal system will break down. Those positive laws have to be seen as deriving from the wills of those subject to them. The obligation to law is derived by agreement. Within a legal system punishment enforces only what is already taken to be unjust.

How does Grotius then define a law of nature? In Grotius's view, 'the law of nature is a dictate of right reason, which points out that an act, according as it is or is not in conformity with rational nature, has in it a quality of moral baseness or moral necessity; and that, in consequence, such an act is either forbidden or enjoined by the author of nature, God'.[30] As Haakonssen notes, natural law is for Grotius essentially moral law.[31] In Grotius's estimation not only are we never wholly free from social rules but these rules form certain types of legal obligation. In his view there are strict legal duties even in the absence of the power to enforce them. These natural (legal) duties derive their authority from God and are binding in virtue of our faith in him. What God wills and what becomes law must accord with reason. Even though God is powerful he cannot make good what is evil. God cannot, in other words, legislate in a way which is contrary to human reason. Although God's authority extends over everything he cannot 'cause that two times two should make four'.[32] The laws of nature are indeed unchangeable 'but the thing in regard to which the law of nature has ordained, undergoes change'.[33] Thus the laws of nature may require different actions from us at different times. So we, as human individuals subject to the laws of nature, must be free to interpret their application in each particular circumstance.

There are two ways of proving that a rule (consistent with Grotius's method) constitutes part of the law of nature: 'Proof *a priori* consists in demonstrating the necessary agreement or disagreement of anything with a rational and social nature; proof *a posteriori*, in concluding, if not with absolute assurance, at least with every probability, that that is according to the law of nature which is believed to be such among all nations, or among all those that are more advanced in civilization.'[34] The second mode of proof is founded ultimately on what Grotius calls the 'common sense of mankind'.[35] The law of nature thus provides the basis both for the law of nations and municipal law. The mode of deriving municipal law therefore has features in common with the mode of deriving the law of nations. 'The proof for the law of nations is similar to that for unwritten municipal law; it is found in unbroken custom as the testimony of those who are skilled in it.'[36] Human law is not necessarily connected with state institutions, extending beyond them both internally and externally: 'Human law is divided into municipal law, law narrower in scope than municipal law, and law broader in scope than municipal law, which is the law of nations.'[37]

THE LAW OF NATIONS AND JUST WAR

The question of the standing of international law is a difficult one. Many have doubted both its reality and its efficacy. Many states' leaders have simply swept to one side considerations of international law when they have perceived their vital interests to be at stake. But equally, many have sought to base their claims to fair or just treatment on an interpretation of international law. Although international law enjoys a different status from domestic law, the case for an entirely sceptical approach cannot be proven. The different status enjoyed by domestic law, particularly in the sphere of enforcement and compliance, may after all only be a difference of degree rather than kind.

Grotius's concern with international law is almost overwhelmingly to do with the problem of war. Grotius wants to regulate war and avert some of its worst consequences. His interest in war is not simply occasional. Grotius wants to minimize and regulate war in general.[38] Grotius's concern with war is similar to that of Kant, if at a less ambitious level. Kant wants to rule out war altogether whereas Grotius wishes to remove its most harmful effects. Kant regards war as the worst of all evils and thinks that from the moral standpoint war should be rejected as a means for resolving social disputes.[39] So wars are incompatible with legality. In this respect Grotius differs from Kant. For Grotius laws are not founded solely on expediency but they are not contrary to it. The laws of nations are to the advantage of nations themselves and attempts to regulate wars are, therefore, advantageous even though those attempts are founded in morality. Just as civil laws can be seen as being in the interest of those who abide by them so natural law is reinforced by considerations of expediency rather than undermined by them. This brings Grotius, by a process of neat deduction, to the law of nations: 'But just as the laws of each state have in view the advantage of that state, so by mutual consent it has become possible that certain laws should originate as between all states, or a great many states; and it is apparent that the laws thus originating had in view the advantage, not of particular states, but of the great society of states. And this is what is called the law of nations, whenever we distinguish that term from the law of nature.'[40]

If states have found it to their advantage to wage war then it is equally the case that they have found it to their advantage to create and respect international laws. The waging of war and the existence of the law of nations are far from being incompatible with one another.[41] 'Least of all should that be admitted', in Grotius's view, 'which some people imagine, that in war all laws are in abeyance. On the contrary war ought not to be undertaken except for the enforcement of rights, it should be carried on only within the bounds of law and good faith.'[42] The municipal laws of states cannot help us with issues of war but the law of nations and the experience of its recognition and acceptance can inform us of the rights we enjoy even when hostilities have broken out.

In arguing in favour of a theory of just war Grotius was building upon a well established tradition. The Christian philosophers and theologians Augustine and Aquinas had argued that on occasions Christian powers and Christian subjects were justified in waging war. But they had not specified very clearly what these occasions were. Aquinas had for instance stressed that the body declaring the war should enjoy proper authority and the intentions of those waging the war should be without malice but there is not a full discussion of the implications of these rules.[43] According to G. D. Draper, 'Grotius made a major advance upon the work done by his predecessors in his detailed and systematic elaboration of the "just causes" of war.'[44] In some respects this step forward is only to be expected since Grotius wished to make the laws relating to war part of the law of nations itself. Here Grotius shows a strong dialectical sense in turning the usual argument against the existence of international law – seemingly offerred by the incidence of violent conflict amongst states – back on itself. Grotius's protagonists could cite war as an example of the way in which justice did not prevail in international relations. This is an argument which is repeated by Hegel who regards international law as 'an ought to be' and describes world history as a sphere beyond justice and right. For Hegel 'international law springs from the relations between autonomous states. It is for this reason that what is in and for itself in the law of nations retains the form of an ought-to-be, since its actuality depends on different wills each of which is sovereign.'[45] But Grotius takes a different position. He argues from the prevalence of war to the existence of the law of nations. War, Grotius regards as a part of the social conduct of states.

The theory of just war plays a crucial part in Grotius's attempt to establish international law. Grotius seems to reason that if he can demonstrate there are grounds for just war then all the prosecutors of war cannot be seen as being on the same legal and moral footing. If in every armed conflict one side represents a just cause and the other an ignoble cause, then one protagonist may be seen as upholding international law and the other may be seen as violating it. In establishing the grounds for just war Grotius is, therefore, in his own view, providing strong evidence for a law of nations. As Draper puts it, 'if war had to be recognized by the law, then it was necessary that war should have a "just cause", as would a lawsuit before a court between citizens within a state'.[46]

Following Draper, Grotius puts forward three main grounds for regarding a war as just and in accord with natural law and the law of nations. They are:

1. Defence against an injury, actual or threatening, but not anticipating;
2. A recovery of what is legally due to the aggrieved state;
3. The infliction of punishment upon the wrongdoing state.[47]

These grounds for just war follow closely what Grotius thinks the individual is entitled to do in the state of nature. In practice Grotius draws no distinction between what individuals are entitled to do in the state of nature and what states are entitled to do because he regards both conditions as the same. States and individuals are always subject to natural law, from which we can deduce both what is required of municipal laws and what is necessary according to the law of nations.

Grotius breaks down the barriers between domestic and international political theory because for him there are no such barriers. Both the domestic sphere and the international sphere belong to the same universal society. Private wars are subject to the same conditions of legality as public wars. As we shall see, there is a somewhat similar argument in Locke where he suggests that war need not be absent from the relations amongst individuals.

CONCLUSION

The historian of political thought, J. N. Figgis, provides a very useful summing up of Grotius's contribution in his perhaps dated, but still interesting and relevant, *Studies of Political Thought from Gerson to Grotius*. Figgis remarks how interesting it is that the Low Countries should produce a political thinker of the first rank, like Grotius, in the seventeenth century. In Figgis's opinion, the Netherlands was one of the most progressive countries in Europe at the time. As he puts it, 'the Netherlands were to the seventeenth what the England of the Revolution was to the eighteenth and early nineteenth centuries, a working model of free institutions'.[48] Grotius's contribution to political theory and international law was founded on his experience in Dutch politics and life. The Netherlands at the time was like the 'University of Europe', it was a rich source of new ideas and new practices. In his account of international law Grotius gave voice to the newly emerging ideas of his time. Although 'the juristic equality of sovereigns was not beginning to be a fact until the close of the sixteenth century', Grotius was able to see that the principle would be in future the foundation of international order.[49] Partly because of his profound understanding of international law and partly because of his experience of Dutch politics Grotius took the view that resistance to a sovereign might only be contemplated under the most extreme of circumstances. If the international order of sovereign states is to function then broad acceptance of the possibility of opposition and internal state revolution must be denied. We cannot have successful captains in leaky ships.

Although Grotius's political ideas might, at a domestic level, be taken to stand in the way of radical progress, as Figgis points out, Grotius's views on international law encouraged beneficial development. 'The fundamental basis of the whole system of Grotius is the claim that men are in a society bound together by a natural law which makes promises binding.'[50] Grotius tries to foster trust not only in relations amongst individuals but also in relations amongst states. 'International law is like schoolboy honour or good form, it does not destroy selfishness or quarrelling or cheating; but it proclaims that certain things are to be avoided and others are obligatory, and it unites even those most sharply divided as members in a single society. It does not solve the problem of man in society, but it recognizes it. Now the theory of Machiavelli and Hobbes at bottom is the reverse of this. It teaches that men are not in society at all except by accident and artifice. With all its superficial attractions it fails to reach the true facts; that even hatred implies a relation, and that neither States nor individuals can have differences unless there be some atmosphere which unites them.'[51] As Figgis notes, Grotius was a brave and early critic of the doctrine of 'raison d'etat'. This is a doctrine which justifies all actions taken by the leaders of states provided those actions are undertaken with a view to the ultimate security of the state. Grotius believes that there are wider systems of values to which states' leaders should adhere going beyond political prudence or expediency. 'The service of Grotius, his forerunners and successors, is not that they produced a scientific system under which State action could be classified, but that they succeeded in placing some bounds to the unlimited predominance of "reason of state".'[52]

A similarly positive assessment of Grotius's political thinking is provided by Richard Tuck in his *Philosophy and Government 1572–1651*. Tuck regards Grotius as an extraordinarily innovative political thinker, especially in the ethical field, and argues that Grotius's contribution to political thought is often under-appreciated. According to Tuck, the 'basis of Grotius's new theory is an account of the moral life in which the priority of self-preservation was balanced by a universal ban on wanton injury, and the two principles were seen as compatible with a very wide range of possible social practices and moral beliefs'.[53] In the manner of the historian of political thought Tuck understands Grotius's novelty primarily in terms of the theory of the state, but Tuck is also aware that Grotius carries through this novelty in his understanding of international life. For Grotius 'social life is the peaceable exercise by each member of his rights, and in particular his fundamental right of self-preservation. It was for this reason that Grotius was able to characterize the relationships between modern states as social, for each state had a set of rights which it could maintain against its neighbours.'[54]

Grotius had experienced at first hand the ups and downs of the European political world. He had also experienced European diplomacy for over a decade or so, albeit in the service of a foreign power. It is encouraging that his conclusions from this experience are not wholly cynical nor without hope for the future. 'The object of Grotius was not to make men perfect or treat them as such, but to see whether there were not certain common duties generally felt as binding, if not always practised, and to set forth an ideal.'[55]

Christien van der Anker has interpreted Grotius in this spirit in order to provide a foundation for a global theory of distributive justice. In my view this takes us beyond a literal understanding of Grotius's project but it is, nonetheless, an interesting way in which to employ Grotius's leading ideas. In van der Anker's opinion, Grotius's assumption of the sociability of human individuals can be used to overcome what she sees as a circularity in many contemporary theories of justice.[56] This circularity she thinks is at least evident in the theories of justice of Jurgen Habermas, John Rawls and Brian Barry. In these theories of justice she believes that morality is defined by 'reference to reasonableness' yet 'reasonableness is (also) explained in terms of morality'.[57] The reference to human sociability, in van der Anker's view, provides a less tautological basis on which to argue for redistribution. 'The Grotian idea of norms rather than bargaining, binding individuals in a society together supports the notion of reasonableness.'[58] In Grotian theory those who wish to find arguments for a fairer distribution of global resources can find an argument which is not based solely on fairness itself.

Van der Anker draws support for this Grotian view from the legal philosophy of H. L. A. Hart. From Hart's work van der Anker draws the idea of a 'minimum content of natural law'.[59] This minimum content she believes is in line with Grotius's account of human society and 'gives a non-meta-physical context to the notion of sociability'.[60] For Hart there are seemingly five elements which make up the minimum content of natural law. These are 'human vulnerability, approximate equality, limited altruism, limited resources and limited understanding and strength of will'.[61] All these factors move individuals towards cooperation. Thus, for van der Anker, it is not too far-fetched to use Grotius's theory of international politics as a foundation for the global redistribution of wealth. Possibly this may represent the direction in which a modern Grotian may want to go, but it amounts to something a good deal more ambitious than Grotius himself was aiming for.

NOTES

1. L. Strauss and J. Cropsey, *History of Political Philosophy*, Chicago University Press, Chicago, 1987, p.386
2. L. Vansomeren, *Umpire to the Nations: Grotius*, Dennis Dobson, London, 1965, p.23

3. C. S. Edwards, *Hugo Grotius: The Miracle of Holland*, Nelson Hall, Chicago, 1981, p.1
4. R. Tuck, 'Grotius and Selden' in J. H. Burns (ed.), *The Cambridge History of Political Thought*, Cambridge University Press, Cambridge, 1994, p.500
5. H. Bull, B. Kingsbury, A. Roberts, *Hugo Grotius and International Relations*, Oxford University Press, Oxford, 1992, p.267
6. Ibid.
7. Ibid., p.93
8. Ibid., p.60
9. S. Buckle, *Natural Law and the Theory of Property*, Oxford University Press, Oxford, 1991, pp.17–18
10. K. Haakonssen, 'Hugo Grotius and the History of Political Thought', *Political Theory*, 13, No. 2, May 1985, p.240
11. Ibid., p.241
12. Ibid., p.244
13. Ibid., p.247
14. S. Buckle, *Natural Law and the Theory of Property*, p.4
15. Ibid., p.5
16. Ibid., p.7
17. H. Grotius, *De Jure Belli ac Pacis Libri Tres* (tr. F. W. Kelley), Oceania Publications, New York, 1964, pp.3–5
18. Ibid., p.4
19. Ibid.
20. Ibid., p.5
21. Ibid., p.9
22. Ibid.
23. Ibid.
24. Ibid., p.20
25. Ibid.: 'To this opinion sometimes John Ferus and my fellow-countryman Erasmus seem to incline, men who have the utmost devotion to peace in both Church and State.'
26. 'Each ruling class makes laws that are in its own interests, a democracy democratic laws, a tyranny tyrannical ones and so on; and in making these laws they define as "right" for their subjects what is in the interest of themselves.' Plato, *The Republic,* Penguin, Harmondsworth, 1972, p.66
27. H. Grotius, *De Jure Belli ac Pacis*, p.11
28. J. Figgis, *Studies of Political Thought from Gerson To Grotius*, Cambridge University Press, Cambridge, p.187
29. H. Grotius, *De Jure Belli ac Pacis*, p.14
30. Ibid., p.39
31. K. Haakonssen, 'Hugo Grotius and the History of Political Thought', p.249: 'At the center of Grotius's idea of natural law is, as already mentioned, the concept of humankind's social nature. It is inherent in our nature or a law of our nature that to live humanly, we should live socially.' Cf. p.240
32. H. Grotius, *De Jure Belli ac Pacis*, p.40
33. Ibid.
34. Ibid., p.42
35. Ibid.
36. Ibid., p.44

37. Ibid.
38. O. Yasuaki, *A Normative Approach to War: peace, war, and justice in Hugo Grotius*, Oxford University Press, Oxford, 1993, p.334
39. I. Kant, *Political Writings*, (ed. H. Reiss, tr. H. B. Nisbet), Cambridge University Press, Cambridge, 1991, p.174; *Akademie Ausgabe*, VI, p.354
40. H. Grotius, *De Jure Belli ac Pacis*, p.15
41. H. Bull, B. Kingsbury, A. Roberts, *Hugo Grotius and International Relations*, p.200
42. H. Grotius, *De Jure Belli ac Pacis*, p.18
43. T. Aquinas, *Selected Political Writings*, Basil Blackwell, Oxford, 1965, pp.159–61
44. H. Bull, B. Kingsbury, A. Roberts, *Hugo Grotius and International Relations*, p.194
45. Hegel, *Philosophy of Right*, Oxford University Press, Oxford, 1969, para. 330, p.212
46. H. Bull, B. Kingsbury, A. Roberts, *Hugo Grotius and International Relations*, p.195
47. Ibid., pp.195–6
48. J. N. Figgis, *Studies of Political Thought from Gerson to Grotius*, p.165
49. Ibid., p.185
50. Ibid., p.186
51. Ibid., p.189
52. Ibid., p.188
53. R. Tuck, *Philosophy and Government 1572–1651*, Cambridge University Press, Cambridge, 1993, p.176
54. Ibid., p.197
55. J. N. Figgis, *Studies of Political Thought*, p.188
56. C. van der Anker, 'The Problem of Circularity in an Impartial Theory of Global Justice', *Contemporary Political Studies*, Vol. 2, Political Studies Association of the United Kingdom, Belfast, 1995, p.774
57. Ibid.
58. Ibid., p.778
59. Ibid., p.779
60. Ibid., p.780
61. Ibid., p.779

7 John Locke and International Politics

'Among critical philosophers Locke deserves priority' – Immanuel Kant[1]

INTRODUCTION

There has been an earlier attempt to characterize Locke's international theory. This is by Richard H. Cox (encouraged by, amongst others, Hans Morgenthau, Leo Strauss and Kenneth Thompson) in *Locke on War and Peace*. Cox gives an account of Locke which makes him appear very close to his fellow English philosopher Thomas Hobbes in his thinking about international politics. According to Cox, Locke was very much concerned about the insecurity and instability of international relations and recommended an extreme watchfulness in foreign policy. Foreign policy takes precedence over domestic policy because it concerns issues on which the survival of the state depends. States have to look to themselves for any enforcement of an international order and cannot afford to be complacent in the preparation of their defences. According to Cox's interpretation of Locke, 'the state of nature between sovereign commonwealths is in fact a vestige of the original state of nature which, so far from being a state of plenty and harmony of interests, is one of extreme penury and conflict'.[2] As a consequence, it may be said that Locke 'views the actual standard of international behaviour as one which is set by the tendency of the least law abiding'.[3] Locke is portrayed as almost as deep a pessimist about the human and international condition as Hobbes. No genuine progress is envisaged in international affairs: 'The state of nature between commonwealths is one of unending though irregular oscillation between actual war and uneasy peace.'[4] A different view is taken here. Locke is seen as a natural law theorist who believes that even in the absence of sovereign authority certain rules of justice are followed by people. As rational beings we are all potentially aware of what these natural rules are and we are not released from an obligation to them simply because there is no neutral authority to enforce them. Thus Locke is much more positive, in my view, about the prospects for international order than Cox implies. Moreover, Locke has a conception of the development of national and international which has been extremely influential. Far from being an advocate of the status quo in domestic and international life, Locke was in fact a strong advocate of change.

Locke's vision of international politics is one of a gradually expanding international civil society, made up of independent civil societies. Civil societies are required to live in peace with one another by following the laws of nature. As Locke sees it, civil societies are ones in which laws of nature are respected and maintained alongside publicly recognized laws. By definition therefore Locke would expect the leaders of civil societies to follow lawful external policies. Of course, Locke does not expect relations between fellow civil societies to be entirely trouble free. Inconveniences and inconsistencies are bound to occur but they should not necessarily lead to war. War between civil societies would represent a failure to live up to the standards of those societies. Were a war to break out, one or both of those societies would have ceased to be civil. So, in Locke's view, civil societies, like rational individuals, are potentially capable of living in peace with one another even if there is no independent third party to enforce rules. Locke's theory of international politics is also dynamic. This dynamism is not so much provided by war and peace but more by a key principle of Locke's internal politics, the principle of property ownership. Locke puts forward a theory of property relations which has expansionist implications. Locke has a view as to how the best forms of social arrangements come into being, underpinning his favoured view of property relations and he believes that this pattern can be repeated world-wide. The implications of this view were most radical in Locke's day for those parts of the globe which were not organized in the civil, representative way he puts forward in his *Two Treatises of Government*, first published in 1690. In essence, Locke's political theory provides a justification for the global expansion of the civil society system, developed first in Europe (particularly Britain), resting on a money economy with the free circulation of commodities. Karl Marx was to call this system capitalism.

Locke's international theory looks upon the earth as a common resource which can be independently exploited for the benefit of each property-owning individual. Locke's theory provides a justification for the prevalent form of western economic and political organization. His thinking is at one with a certain kind of capitalist expansion. I suggest that it harmonizes best with the kind of market economy and external economic links developed by the United States of America. As such, Locke's theory demonstrates most of the benefits and many of the drawbacks associated with the global expansion of United States society. As well as pointing out the problematic aspects of this expansionist theory I shall try also to highlight its strengths.

The most important aspects of Locke's political thinking are his theory of property and his theory of political representation. The two theories are intimately connected. Representative government, for Locke, has to be brought into being in order fully to safeguard property. Without a representative form of government the retention of property is difficult, inconvenient, although not wholly impossible.

On the face of it property relations and representative government are not central topics for international relations. But as this chapter will try to show this is a very superficial view. Property relations and representative government lie at the heart of international relations, not least because representative governments are a dominating force in contemporary international politics and because in general they favour certain types of property relations. Those property relations are often very close to the those advocated by John Locke in his *Two Treatises of Government*. At present the major power in international politics is the United States and its political practice and ideology have been strongly influenced by the political philosophy of John Locke.

Like many other early modern political philosophers Locke thought about problems of political order in terms of the concept of the state of nature. A state of nature is a condition of human life prior to social organization. The concept also figures prominently in the political philosophies of Thomas Hobbes and Jean-Jacques Rousseau. The particular kind of social organization that Locke and his fellow political philosophers were anxious to see develop was that of a *civil society*. Civil society such philosophers identified with the existence of law and settled property relations. In Locke's view human interaction was not without laws in the state of nature. However, these laws were not properly codified nor were there institutions that could effectively implement them. These laws were laws ordained by God. Locke calls them the laws of nature. Some of these laws ordained by God were already revealed to us through his servants but many others we (as God's property) had to work our for ourselves through the use of our reason. Locke shared with thinkers like Thomas Aquinas the belief that the use of reason by individuals would lead to a common understanding of what the law required in any particular instance. Thus in the state of nature there should not be any grave or insuperable problems in understanding what the law should be in any particular instance. Individuals endowed by God with a common reason would see what the relevant rules were. Problems might arise only in the implementation of those rules, since in the state of nature there would only be interested parties in any particular conflict. In the absence of regulating political institutions there would be no properly neutral powers to adjudge disputes.

As we have seen in the previous chapter, this natural law assumption is a very brave and commendable one but it is not one that is now often held in its original sense. It is one Locke took for granted.[5] Philosophers are nowadays very rightly cautious about claiming a common reason. Knowledge of the languages and cultures of other people have led commentators to take a more relativistic view of the nature of justice, and has helped undermine the notion that there is any natural right. Even in Locke's time it seems fairly clear that each interpreter was inclined to produce their own particular version of God's laws. Locke's *Two Treatises of Government* was after all occasioned by a dispute with Robert Filmer about the supposed divine right of kings.

Interestingly Locke considers this relativist argument but only to disregard it: 'Men are everywhere met with, not only a select few and those in a private station, but whole nations, in whom no sense of law, no moral rectitude, can be observed. There are also other nations, and they are many, which with no guilty feeling disregard some at least of the precepts of natural law and consider it to be not only customary but also praiseworthy to commit, and to approve of, such crimes as are utterly loathsome to those who think rightly and live according to nature. Hence among these nations, thefts are lawful and commendable, and the greedy hands of robbers are not debarred from violence and injury by any shackles of conscience. For others there is no disgrace in debauchery; and while in one place there are no temples or altars of the gods, in another they are found splattered with human blood. Since such is the case, it may be justly doubted whether the law of nature is binding on all mankind, unsettled and uncertain as men are, accustomed to the most diverse institutions, and driven by impulses in quite opposite directions; for that the decrees of nature are so obscure that they are hidden from whole nations is hard to believe.'[6] Yet, 'in spite of these objections, we maintain that the binding force of natural law is perpetual and universal'.[7] The evidence seems to suggest that it is Locke's deep faith in God that leads him to this optimistic conclusion.

THE STATE OF NATURE AND THE STATE OF WAR

Like his earlier contemporary Thomas Hobbes, John Locke (1632–1704) thinks that human individuals consent to establishing government over themselves. Locke sees this as a relinquishing of a natural condition of freedom, so that we can enjoy greater certainty and prosperity under the rule of a sovereign. Sovereignty Locke sees as arising voluntarily and alongside the sovereignty of other states.

However, there are many respects in which Locke differs from Hobbes in his view of what individuals are naturally like. Hobbes takes a stark view of human nature as narrowly egoistic and combative. In general Locke takes what we might see as a more optimistic view of our original or natural qualities outside civil society. As he sees it, we are not necessarily at each others' throats in a state of nature. Indeed, we may well flourish outside a settled civil condition. But this does not necessarily make it preferable to an organized society.

In his account of the state of nature Locke starts with the assumption that individuals in this condition are 'at perfect freedom to order their actions, and dispose of their possessions and persons as they think fit'.[8] This is, of course, a condition of complete equality where no one enjoys any more power than anyone else. Unlike Hobbes, though, Locke does not see this as leading to a complete absence of discipline. Though this natural condition may be a state of liberty, Locke says, 'it is not a state of licence'.[9] Locke believes that there are laws which hold in the state of nature, laws which are derived from God. These laws do not require the existence of an effective political sovereign to be valid.

In the absence of an effective political sovereign God requires of us that we respect the freedom and independence of others. Locke sees us all as the property of a one divine Being and we should recognize this common quality in our mutual relations. Just as much as we ourselves desire not to have our freedom and security impaired, so we ought not to invade the freedom and security of others. In this natural state, therefore, the freedom of the one individual is dependent upon the reciprocal acceptance of the freedom of the other. Here we enjoy no authority to subordinate another individual to our own purposes.

A corollary of everybody being allowed to enjoy their freedom is that everyone has the authority to defend themselves if attacked, and to punish another person for infringing our natural rights. This follows automatically from the perfect equality of individuals who are in a state of nature. If there is no certainty as to who, or what institution, enjoys authority we have to see to it ourselves that the law is observed. So it is 'that every man in the state of nature has a power to kill a murderer'[10] or to punish a person to that degree which accords with the magnitude of the crime.

Locke, then, sees our natural state as unstable and politically unsatisfactory. For the law to be effective it has to be implemented by the individual. Each retains the right to be a judge in their own case. This is an inconvenient state of affairs, but it is not as inhospitable and without security as someone like Hobbes imagines it to be. In contrast with Hobbes, for example, Locke believes individuals can hold on to their possessions and thus own property in the state of nature. Locke expects that individuals will, in their own ultimate interest, respect each other's natural right to make things into their own. Under natural law there is an obligation to come to the assistance of another individual threatened by breaches of the law. We might also see this as applying to states when one of their number is subject to aggression. Locke would envisage the possibility of intervention to uphold natural and international law, but this obligation to help would not require an individual or state to endanger their own survival. Hobbes would not accept this view. As Hobbes sees it, there is no security in the state of nature and, therefore, there is no property nor obligation to defend it.[11]

Locke would argue that Hobbes in the *Leviathan* confuses two fundamentally different types of human condition. Locke believes that there is an important distinction to be made between the 'state of nature' and the 'state of war'. Of course, this distinction is not only extremely important for Locke's theory of civil society but also for his account of international politics. In Locke's view, a state of war is brought about by one individual seeking to bring another under his absolute power. It must be assumed that a person who tries to bring another into this condition has one design only, namely, the enslavement of the other person. Slavery, Locke sees as contrary to man's natural freedom and, therefore, contrary to the laws of nature. 'The natural liberty of man is to be free from any superior power on earth, and not to be under the will or legislative authority of man, but to have only the law of nature for his rule.'[12] As slavery rests upon arbitrary force Locke regards it as contrary to what God wills for the human species. Slavery therefore does not properly belong to the international order.

What properly belongs to the international order belongs also to the state of nature. Contrary to the view taken by Hobbes this state of nature is not a state of war. For Locke a state of war brings arbitrary force into play which can only have subjugation as its aim. Force, Locke says, 'or a declared design of force upon the person of another, where there is no common superior on earth to appeal to for relief, is the state of war'.[13] In contrast, 'men living together according to reason without a common superior on earth, with no authority to judge between them, is properly the state of nature'.[14] What is significant about the state of war for Locke is that it can occur even within the social condition: 'Want of a common judge with authority puts all men in a state of nature; force without right upon a man's person makes a state of war both where there is, and is not, a common judge.'[15] A thief who wants to rob me of my possessions puts me just as much into a state of war, as the state which attacks the state to which I belong. The difference between the two incidents Locke sees as a difference of degree rather than kind. War, as Locke understands it, upsets our natural condition rather than reflects it.

The clash with Hobbes's views on this issue could not be more marked. For Hobbes 'it is manifest, that during that time men live without a common power to keep them in awe, they are in that condition which is called war; and such a war, as is of every man, against every man'.[16] The state of nature, the state of war and the normal condition of international relations are one and the same thing for Hobbes. This is not so with Locke. For Locke the state of nature is no more than an inconvenient condition where disputes unavoidably arise because of the lack of a common authority. As Locke put it, 'the state of nature has a law of nature to govern it, which obliges every one, and reason, which is that law, teaches all mankind who will but consult it, that being all equal and independent, no one ought to harm another in his life, health, liberty or possessions ... And, being furnished with like faculties, sharing all in one community of nature, there cannot be supposed any such subordination among us that may authorise us to destroy one another, as if we were made for one another's uses, as the inferior ranks of creatures are for ours'.[17] Locke uses his account of the state of nature to put forward his doctrine of Christian universalism and humanism. This Christian universalism applies not only to our relationship with other individuals in the absence of a common authority but also to the relations among states. Hobbes respects this doctrine but believes that it is sadly inoperative in the state of nature.

There is a conflict then between Locke and Hobbes about the depth of the problems posed by the absence of a settled sovereign authority. For Hobbes it implies hostility and incipient war, but for Locke the consequences are less drastic: it implies possible disruption and inconvenience. With Hobbes in the state of nature we are out in the cold, for Locke in the state of nature we are out in the warm with the occasional stiff breeze.

But Locke agrees with Hobbes that it is better to move out of the state of nature than to remain with its uncertainties. The device Locke thinks individuals should use to extricate themselves from the state of nature is the social contract. To avoid the complexities and inconvenience of each person being his or her own judge every individual consents with others 'to make one body politic under one government'.[18] This government provides the members of the society with the certainty they require that the laws will be enforced. The government is in turn provided with a great deal of authority over the individual member because the individual has voluntarily created the sovereign authority. A key element in Locke's political theory is that he attempts to derive our political obligations from our own voluntary agreements and actions. The authority that states enjoy over us can, for Locke, be seen as an authority we have vested in them which is an authority which should always be compatible with our common humanity. Representative government which incorporates our agreement (and the possibility of dissent) provides this kind of authority.

This helps explain the preoccupation of the first book of Locke's *Two Treatises of Government*. In this book Locke sets out to prove that Robert Filmer's claim that the authority of government is based on the divine right of kings to rule. Locke finds that neither history nor reason substantiate Filmer's royalist claim. Political power has to be distinguished from the patriarchal power which God vested in Adam and which Filmer believes passed on to the human race as a whole. A social contract had to be presupposed if we are to have a legitimate sovereign. This social contract removes us from the state of nature.

Interestingly, although both Locke and Hobbes think we have to leave our natural condition as individuals neither believes that states should do the same. For Hobbes it is essential for the persistence of civilization that we should abandon our natural condition as individuals, for Locke the step is not quite so critical but it is nonetheless rationally indispensable. Yet the equivalent step at the international level is not recommended. This is possibly easier to explain with Locke since, according to his view, the absence of a common authority does not undermine law altogether. With Locke natural law remains in force, even in the absence of a neutral power of enforcement. Locke is content to see international life continue in the natural condition since he thinks it may still lead to a kind of order. With Hobbes the situation is different. Hobbes should, on the face of it, press the notion of an international sovereign very strongly. But this is not so. He estimates that the lack of order which results at an international level will not be as damaging as the lack of order at an individual level.[19]

PROPERTY AS THE UNIVERSAL HUMAN CONDITION

Locke establishes a tradition of thinking about property relations which sees them as lying at the heart of human existence. He argues that we cannot be human individuals in the full sense unless we own property. From this point of view property is not only for the privileged few but is the right of every free person. But property ownership is not only important for the individual. Property relations take us to the heart of social relations in general. Property relations determine the way in which income and wealth are acquired and distributed. For Locke property relations are more basic than political arrangements. Indeed, in his view, the main rationale for political arrange-ments at all is to safeguard property relations.

Locke has a view of property relations which transcends political boundaries. His theory of property is intended to be of universal application. His account of property leads to a theory of political arrangements not for one particular society but a theory of political arrangements for society in general. The stress which Locke puts upon the primacy of property relations makes him into a global (political) theorist.

C. B. Macpherson has controversially described Locke's theory of property as the 'theory of possessive individualism'. Macpherson regards Hobbes as the best example of such a theorist but 'as with Hobbes, Locke's deduction starts with the individual and moves out to society and the state, but, again as with Hobbes, the individual with which he starts has already been created in the image of market man. Individuals are by nature equally free from the jurisdiction of others. The human essence is freedom from any relations other than those a man enters with a view to his own interest. The individual's freedom is rightly limited only by the requirements of others' freedom. The individual is proprietor of his own person, for which he owes nothing to society. He is free to alienate his capacity to labour, but not his whole person. Society is a series of relations between proprietors. Political society is a contractual device for the protection of proprietors and the orderly regulation of their relations.'[20] Macpherson's interpretation of Locke and Hobbes is somewhat controversial in that Macpherson implies that Locke and Hobbes's main, but somewhat obscured motivation, was to provide a defence of capitalist accumulation. Macpherson therefore sees Locke's theory of property in a morally problematic light as a theory of acquisitive individualism.

The main thrust of Macpherson's argument is, however, interesting and illuminating. Locke sets out to justify the acquisition of property in the strongest possible terms. As Macpherson argues, Locke connects property with human freedom and this freedom should be universal. Political institutions should develop from property relations and their main purpose is to allow property relations to flourish. The social contract which establishes political relations amongst individuals should grow from the already existing relations between proprietors. Any political arrangements which grow from the social contract are subject to revision and alteration by the proprietors who establish the contract in the first place. So government is seen as a device which is at the service of individuals rather than simply a mechanism which subjects them to control.

Locke's theory of property belongs to capitalist society in the earliest stages of its development. The theory belongs to a period where there was, in my view, no doubt as to the progressive nature of the new economic order. In Europe the power of the feudal aristocracy, based upon ownership of the land, was being broken up by a new class of urban financiers and entrepreneurs. It is not surprising, therefore, that Locke should see a great deal of virtue in the individual acquisition of property because it was a principle of social advance whose advantageous effects he could observe for himself. Locke had no desire to bolster a decaying aristocracy by criticizing the personal acquisition of property.

Locke believes that the ownership of property is compatible with the laws of nature. Significantly also he believes the expansive, overseas acquisition of property is compatible with nature and God's wishes. He disputes Hobbes's view that it is not possible to own property outside civil society. As Locke sees it, the ownership of property is possible in the state of nature. Locke thinks we have to assume that the things of nature are capable of becoming our property otherwise we should never satisfy our needs. The most primitive of individuals need to eat. There has to be a way whereby what they consume can become theirs. Locke accepts that the earth was originally given to mankind in common, yet now within civil societies it is owned in an unequal way by individuals. How does he see this coming about? To answer this problem Locke puts forward what might be described as a 'labour theory of property'. In brief, Locke thinks we establish property rights in things by mixing our labour with them. In Locke's view, our control and use of nature are our title to its produce. Locke's first assumption in trying to establish this is significant. He suggests that 'though the earth and all inferior creatures be common to all men yet every man has a "property" in his own "person"'.[21] This is underpinned by the religious view that we are all God's property and as part of his settlement of the human species on earth we are entitled to regard ourselves as the owners of our own bodies. From this assumption that our limbs belong to us Locke moves on to claim that those things we shape with our hands, such as the products of our labour, also belong to us.

Locke therefore believes that our property rights are established by our labour in the state of nature. There is no need for the consent of any other person for us to own those things we take from nature. 'Whatsoever, then, he removes out of the state of nature hath provided and left it in, he hath mixed his labour with it, and joined to it something that is his own, and thereby made it his property'.[22] Because the individual has removed an object from nature by his labour it justly belongs to him. This property can only be alienated to others voluntarily.

It is vital for Locke's theory that we see property as a right which exists prior to any settled society in the state of nature. He thinks that neither a social contract nor government is necessary to make property a reality. For 'if such a consent as that was necessary, man had starved, notwithstanding the plenty God had given him'.[23] To assume that what we have gathered, grown or nurtured is ours solely through robbery or theft is entirely contrary to justice. For Locke there is little doubt, as he prosaically puts it, 'the grass my horse has bit, the turfs my servant has cut, and the ore I have digged in any place, where I have a right to them in common with others, become my property without the assignation or consent of anybody'.[24]

There is a strongly international dimension to this outline of our natural right to property. Locke seems particularly to have in mind the situation in North America at the time of his writing in the late seventeenth century. Locke had strong connections with North America, at one time occupying a post dealing with the colonization of Carolina. As James Tully has pointed out, the European-Amerindian context is especially important in understanding the way in which Locke presents his theory of property.[25] In America property rights were being established by European settlers through settlement and cultivation. These property rights were contrary to the established patterns of cultivation and settlement practised by the American Indians. But Locke sees no difficulty in the founding of the settlers' property rights because of the emphasis he places on the role of labour in establishing entitlement. The settler was perfectly entitled to make into his property whatever he could appropriate through his industry. Locke appears to think his argument is incontrovertible: 'Though the water running in the fountain be every one's, yet who can doubt but that in the pitcher is his only who drew it out? His labour has taken it out of the hands of Nature where it was common, and belonged equally to all her children, and hath thereby appropriated it to himself.'[26] It is only reasonable to expect that we can acquire property in the state of nature such as that obtained in seventeenth-century America. Having something as yours is the basis on which one can use it or consume it. A natural law which prevented the ownership of property would be a contradiction. The American settlers and their frontiersmen have their natural spokesman in Locke.

Although we have a natural right to acquire property we are, in the state of nature, limited to what we can hold. It would be unjust, Locke thinks, for everybody to grab as much as one can in the absence of settled government and law. In these circumstances we have to bear in mind the amount of property we can in fact usefully employ. 'Nothing', Locke holds, 'was made by God for man to spoil or destroy.'[27] So whatever in this condition is more than we need does not rightfully belong to us. In the state of nature, as Locke sees it, we are obligated to restrain our greed and must acquire only enough to satisfy our wants.

This rule also applies to the acquisition of land. To lay claim to large tracts of land we cannot possibly cultivate ourselves is contrary to the laws of nature. Rather 'as much land as a man fills, plants, improves, cultivates, and can use the product of, so much is his property. He by his labour does, as it were, enclose it from the common.'[28] In this condition our ownership and entitlement to things extends only as far as our industry. What entitles us to have things in our possession is that we have laboured upon them in order to make them what they presently are. It goes without saying that what we have no time to work on and transform, we have no right to call our own.

This is a theory of property acquisition that goes well with colonial expansion, particularly the kind of colonialism Locke was familiar with in North America. The labour entitlement to property on the one hand helpfully limits the claims that can be made to ownership by the native nomadic population and, on the other hand, provides a useful basis to the claims of the colonizers to the land they have cultivated and the settlements they erected. The native inhabitants made use of the natural resources available to them in their territories, but not in such a way that they could establish a permanent entitlement to all the land and resources. As Locke would see it, they lived in a condition of plenty which allowed others to come along and make legitimate claims to ownership as well. If everyone observes the rules of nature that reason dictates no great conflicts should ensue in this pre-civil condition.

In the state of nature there is a rough equality in the amount of property each individual is able to own because of the requirement that our acquisitions be limited to what will not spoil. But economic development does not remain at this level. The situation is transformed by the invention of money. Where there is no money a person's wealth is limited to what the person can usefully employ. In our natural condition there is no sense in acquiring more than you can use. Since most useful things are perishable (food in particular) they would only waste. But what takes the human individual out of the state of nature and into civil society is the use of money. One valuable quality of money is that it provides an almost imperishable store of wealth. In Locke's day the role of money was primarily taken on by the precious metals gold and silver. Gold and silver only deteriorate slowly on exposure to the atmosphere, for all practicable purposes they are imperishable stores of wealth. They can also be broken up into the smallest of pieces so they can also play the role of universal equivalent necessary to money.

Gold and silver, once they circulate as money, provide a means whereby the human species can prevent from perishing wealth it cannot immediately use. In Locke's view, this is how inequality in property ownership comes about from the state of nature (where we are all equal). Although on the surface this inequality seems contrary to natural justice Locke thinks it is a change in social and economic relations humans themselves sanction. In his view, human beings give their tacit consent to establishing material inequalites when they accept money relations: 'But since gold and silver, being little useful to the life of man, in proportion to food, raiment, and carriage, has its only value from the consent of men – whereof labour yet makes in great part the measure – it is plain that the consent of men have agreed to a disproportionate and unequal possession of the earth – I mean out of bounds of society and compact.'[29] Within a civil society the amount of inequality is regulated by governments and laws, outside the civil society regulation is provided by the laws of nature and the acceptance and use of money.

Here we can see that Locke's labour theory of property not only sanctions the original acquisition of things but also provides a justification for the worldwide ownership of private property. The expansion of the acceptance and recognition of property goes side by side, as he sees it, with the growth and the extension of the use of money. Another way of putting this is to say that as capitalist economic relations develop, and are extended to all parts of the globe, they carry with them the implicit justification of inequality of wealth and income. This justification applies even in the absence of a developed civil society. A developed civil society can subsequently sanction with positive law the unequal relations that have already appeared. Colonialism and the expansion of European market society to the rest of the world do not need to be added to Locke's theory of property – they are already an integral part of his doctrine. As Ruth Grant puts it, 'far from considering colonization as aggression, Locke considers it a practice that increases "the common stock of mankind" (2nd Treatise, para. 37) by developing and exploiting the productive capacity of the earth'.[30] So colonization and Locke's theory of property go hand in hand: 'There can be no objection to the morality of English colonization of America, for example, if one accepts Locke's argument concerning the manner in which land comes to be property.'[31]

'OF CONQUEST': A LIBERAL THEORY OF INTERNATIONAL RELATIONS

Locke's political theory as a whole may also be taken as a theory of international relations. His account of political relations is also implicitly an account of international relations. His theory of property is, for example, a theory which is intended to have worldwide application and was often read and interpreted as such. One chapter in his *Second Treatise of Government* though is expressly devoted to a topic that is immediately recognizable as falling within the sphere of international relations, namely, chapter 16 which is entitled 'Of Conquest'. As we would expect, this chapter is not out of place in Locke's general discussion of government, focusing as it does on patriarchal theories of political authority which attempt to derive political authority from past subordination. Locke has in mind, in particular, the work of Robert Filmer which seeks to defend the divine right of kings. Locke's main objective in this chapter is to show that a policy of conquest which aims at a permanent right of subjugation over other people is contrary to natural law. In demonstrating this Locke thinks he will have shown that patriarchal claims that we owe allegiance to those who through custom, habit or age seek to dominate individuals are misguided.

In the course of his criticism of the abuse of the right of conquest Locke develops his view of a less hierarchical political and interstate order. Locke's theory was to be particularly influential, connected as his ideas were to be with the American War of Independence and the establishment of the republican system of government in the United States.[32] It is an influence that is still with us. As James Tully puts it, 'three hundred years after its publication the *Two Treatises* continues to present one of the major political philosophies of the modern world' in that 'it provides a set of concepts we standardly use to represent and reflect on contemporary politics'.[33] Locke's opposition to the policy of conquest and hereditary political title became embedded in the political thinking of the new state and subsequently informed United States practice, not only in internal policy but also in external policy. This opposition to a policy of conquest is not only a negative doctrine. In its positive implications it represents a significant, if rudimentary, theory of international society.

A first principle of that theory of international society is that the origins of any form of political association should be regarded as voluntary. Politics should be founded on the people's consent, 'yet such have been the disorders ambition has filled the world with, that in the noise of war, which makes so great a part of the history of mankind, this consent is little taken notice of; and, therefore, many have mistaken the force of arms for the consent of the people, and reckon conquest as one of the originals of government. But conquest is as far from setting up any government as demolishing a house is from building a new one in the place.'[34] Conquest does not create legitimacy. At best legitimacy can arise when a government first set in place by conquest regains the consent of the people. But the title to government derives not from the conquest but from the consent subsequently won.

Although Locke rules out a policy of conquest he does not rule out a possible right of conquest. But this right of conquest does not arise in relation to a normal commonwealth. The right arises only in relation to aggressive powers who seek to impose their will on other states by the use of force. In relation to an aggressor there is a natural right to resort to war. Aggressors by their actions put themselves beyond the normal intercourse of states. Aggression is never justified by the power or size of a state. 'That the aggressor, who puts himself into the state of war with another, and unjustly invades another man's right, can, by such an unjust war, never come to have a right over the conquered, will be easily agreed by all men.'[35]

Locke's account of the state of nature and the importance he attaches to natural law demonstrate that he does not regard war as a normal condition of international relations. The distinction he makes between the state of war and the state of nature implies that war for him is a disruption of the standard relations of individuals and states to one another. 'Thus conquerors' swords often cut up governments by the roots, and mangle societies to pieces, separating the subdued or scattered multitude from the protection of and dependence on that society which ought to have preserved them from violence. The world is too well instructed in, and too forward to allow this way of dissolving governments, to need any more to be said of it.'[36] Locke equates war with the condition of the beast whereas the human condition is one in which reason prevails. There may have been one time where a policy of arbitrary conquest was accepted by individuals and societies but that time is long since over. A deliberate policy of war belongs in Locke's estimation to the infancy of humankind and not to the more advanced condition of his day. It is possible to participate in a just war to deter or punish an aggressor but the war is justified only to counter an initial lapse in the proper condition of human relations. Thus Locke's objection to a policy of conquest also suggests that a main principle of foreign policy should be to retain peaceful relations with other states that act in accordance with natural law. Both reason and experience tell us that civil societies should respect each others' independence. As Cox puts it, ' rulers can never legitimately use the public force in war against the people of another society for the purpose of subjugating them'.[37]

Locke also believes that the traditional inhabitants of a civil society in a settled and cultivated territory shaped by human industry have a right of self-determination. Locke would not extend this right to nomadic peoples nor other peoples without established forms of work and industry. But for those who enjoy such a Western European style of life there exists a right only to be ruled by a government of their choice. If this right is lost through conquest it may nonetheless be legitimately restored, if not by the present generation then by future generations. Locke accepts that a conquered people may have very little power to realize their aim of legitimate self-government. But he argues ingenuously that 'they may appeal' still 'to Heaven, and repeat their appeal till they have recovered the native right of their ancestors'.[38]

Locke has very little to say in his *Two Treatises of Government* about the rights of states and individuals in war, but he does have a great deal to say about rights after war. He warns that victors in a war to counter aggression get no power by conquest over those that conquer with them. States that participate with others in subjugating an aggressor are entitled to a share of the spoils of war and to a control of part of the territory conquered.[39] No superior right can be given to the sovereign of the state which takes the lead in the prosecution of the lawful war. This applies not only to other states but also to those who assist the sovereign from its own territory. Success in war does not accord to the sovereign absolute rule over its own people.

Equally, not everyone in the conquered territory can be treated in an arbitrary way. The spoils of war are limited to an absolute control over those who first raised the sword against the peaceful order. Where the aggression was not supported by the people they are entitled to remain free. Non-combatants are all presumed 'innocent'.[40] The absolute power of the conqueror affects the combatant only and does not extend to his property or his family and descendants. Rightful conquest implies that possession passes not to the conqueror but to the combatant's next of kin. The father's guilt does not necessarily pass to his children 'who may be rational and peaceable, notwithstanding the brutishness and injustice of the father'. 'His goods which Nature, that willeth the preservation of all mankind as much as possible, hath made to belong to the children to keep them from perishing, do still continue to belong to his children.'[41] In the initial stages of conquest a victorious power may get away with flouting these rules of nature, but as time passes such action will only sow the seeds of a just rebellion. The conqueror's duty once the former unjust regime has been destroyed is to help create within the captured territories a civil form of government. Once a people have made reparations and restored a lawful government there is no longer any right to rule over them. Where foreign rule persists without justification no wrong is committed when the people revolt: 'whence it is plain that shaking off a power which force, and not right, hath set over any one, though it hath the name of rebellion, yet is no offence before God'.[42]

CONCLUSION

Locke's theory of international relations represents a fascinating alternative to that of Hobbes. On the whole, Locke stresses the more tranquil aspects of human relations. Like Grotius, Locke draws upon natural law theory to found his view of civil society. This natural law exists prior to states and the interstate system. With Hobbes natural law is only effective after the state has been founded. Before this time natural law simply represents desirable but unattainable ideals. For Locke and Grotius, natural law inheres in human relations from their inception.

Locke's theory of international relations is expansionist. The positive side of worldwide capitalist development is underpinned by Locke's account of government. When put into practice the theory leads to a transformation of traditional forms of cultivation and pastoral life. The introduction of exclusive property rights to the exploitation of natural resources leads to the parcelling out of land and production for a profit. This economically aggressive side of Locke's theory has led to criticism. He has been upbraided for being a defender of bourgeois property rights. But Locke's doctrine is also one of civic expansion which favours, as well as capitalist property rights, liberal political institutions and representative governments. Locke encourages these representative governments to live in peace with one another.

It can also be argued that Locke's political theory led to the spread of a liberal political culture throughout the world and an economic system which led to much higher standards of life. The commercial spirit which goes hand in hand with Locke's political theory led to improved communications and undermined other, less equal social relations. Quite often traditional societies were largely stagnant and, in many instances, barbaric. The least that can be said of Locke's theory is that its adoption created new and, for some, unimagined opportunities.

Locke's theory of representative government is not by any means a docile one. An implication of the theory is that there is a natural right for inhabitants of a territory to attempt to undermine their government if it is not civil in form. Those who possess civil governments therefore provide encouragement to the members of other societies to form their own. The implication of Locke's thinking is that civil representative governments work best with other civil representative governments. States, in taking their place alongside other modern civil states, have to accept the rules of membership of a worldwide civil society which forbids aggression and encourages the acceptance of natural law dictated by reason. Potentially, as Locke's system of international relations expands it would lead to a more peaceful world. If we identify this system of international relations with the one favoured by the external policy of the United States of America, with its Lockean constitution, then there is an argument which favours this view. But the question which arises now is whether with the collapse of communism, and the development of an oligopolistic world capitalism, the limits of the expansion of Locke's system have not been reached? Might not Francis Fukuyama's boast of the universal acceptance of the superiority of the liberal democratic model of political organization represent the fulfilment of Locke's vision? Can we be sure though that this liberal democratic model will guarantee peace? Locke's view of the human being and human society is very much orientated to production. He takes an acquisitive view of the human individual who will always want more rather than less. Also this acquisition is not achieved in isolation. Locke's model of acquisition is competitive with money as the final arbiter in the game. Possibly Locke's model does not fully address the problems of an over-exploited and arguably over-populated globe. Contemporary green theory and cooperative theories of global commerce and industry might seem to suggest so.

In the contemporary global context there are maybe strong grounds to reconsider the applicability of Locke's expansionist theory. As Daniel Bromley suggests in *Environment and Economy*, possibly Kant's more collectively based theory of property (stressing the common element of consent implied by all forms of property right) represents a better model with which to contemplate the future. In Bromley's view, 'the conventional Lockean understanding posits a too-restrictive and improperly dyadic notion of property rights. That is, the Locke-inspired position has individual property rights stand as the last bastion against a meddlesome state.' It prevents one from taking a responsible attitude to the environment. 'This dyadic perspective – the individual versus the state – is, almost by design, one that impedes social change.' Locke's model is insufficiently cooperative. 'While life, in general, would be much more agreeable if there were no need for institutional change, reality is not inclined to cooperate. Population growth creates ever-increasing needs for sewage treatment, for solid waste-disposal, for more highways and housing departments, and for myriad goods and services seemingly prerequisite to the good life. Technology too is advancing in ways that are not always benign for environmental integrity. Finally, as individuals – and nations – become wealthier, tastes and preferences change in a way that attaches greater significance to non-material consumption. As a result, a quiet meadow, a scenic sunset, or a tranquil day at the water gains in value relative to rather more conventional commodities. An environmental economics – and a perspective on property rights – that starts from Lockean statics' may represent 'an analytical dead-end'.[43]

NOTES

1. I. Kant, *Lectures on Logic*, Cambridge University Press, Cambridge, 1992, p.24
2. R. H. Cox, *Locke on War and Peace*, Oxford University Press, Oxford, 1960, p.188
3. Ibid., p.192
4. Ibid., p.171

5.   J. Locke, *Essays on the Law of Nature*, tr. and ed. W. Von Leyden, Oxford University Press, Oxford, p.123

6.   Ibid., p.191

7.   Ibid., p.193

8.   J. Locke, *Two Treatises of Government*, Dent, London, 1977, p.118

9.   Ibid., p.119

10. Ibid., p.122

11. T. Hobbes, *The Leviathan*, Fontana, London, 1969, p.143

12. J. Locke, *Two Treatises*, p.127. No one would choose to be a slave. Locke's attitude to slavery is discussed in detail by Wayne Glauser in 'Three approaches to Locke and the Slave Trade', *Journal of the History of Ideas*, 51, 2, 1990, pp.199–216.

13. J. Locke, *Two Treatises*, p.126

14. Ibid.

15. Ibid., p.127

16. T. Hobbes, *Leviathan*, p.143

17. J. Locke, *Two Treatises*, pp.119–20. It might be argued that this interpretation of the role of the state of nature in Locke's political philosophy underplays the inconveniences that are experienced by individuals or nations in this condition. In other words, it is suggested that although Richard Cox exaggerates the extent to which there is common ground between Locke and Hobbes my interpretation tends to over-emphasize the differences. According to this view, which has been put to me by Geraint Parry, conflict is always a strong possibility with Locke's view of the state of nature. In effect, whilst each individual or state can know the general principles of natural law or international law and thus ought to follow them each may interpret the law in its own interests. So recognition of the *principle* of territorial property rights is compatible with sharp differences over application. For example, both the United Kingdom and Argentina may recognize the principle of a property right based upon the first mixing of 'national labour' with a tract of land but dispute the facts. Lacking a neutral world authority each could properly employ force to secure what it considered its rights under the law and demand compensation (the level of which should be 'proportionate' – but that too could be disputed). Locke also permits self-defence, of course, and this might include regarding theft (loss of territory) as a threat to life (national existence).
     There is a great deal of merit in this argument but there is, in my view, little point to Locke's natural law theory unless he believes there are ways of overcoming these inconveniences without war. It is certainly true that the natural law position he advocates leads to indeterminacies, but Locke would suggest that those indeterminacies are not unlike those experienced in trying to implement and adjudge the law in a civil society. It is misleading to contrast an apparently straightforward implementation of law within states with a thoroughly confused and complex implementation of law between states. Both can be equally tricky.

18. J. Locke, *Two Treatises*, p.165

19. T. Hobbes, *Leviathan*, pp.309–10

20. C. B. Macpherson, *A Theory of Possessive Individualism*, Oxford University Press, Oxford, 1967, p.269

21. J. Locke, *Two Treatises*, p.130

22. Ibid.
23. Ibid. Locke's view that property rights exist prior to the consent of society raises the interesting question of aboriginal rights. Kant's apparent rejection of such rights is discussed by J. Tully in *An Approach to Political Philosophy: Locke in Contexts*, Cambridge University Press, Cambridge, 1993, pp.137–76
24. J. Locke, *Two Treatises*, p.131
25. J. Tully, *An Approach to Political Philosophy*, pp.139–40
26. J. Locke, *Two Treatises*, p.131
27. Ibid.
28. Ibid., p.132
29. Ibid., p.140
30. R. Grant, *John Locke's Liberalism*, Chicago University Press, Chicago, 1987, p.159
31. Ibid., pp.159–60
32. 'It is in Locke's work that one finds the true integration into one edifice, and hence the full exploration of the meaning, of the three most important pillars supporting the Founders' [of the United States] moral vision. Nature or "Nature's God", "property", or the "pursuit of happiness", and the dignity of the individual as a rational human being, parent and citizen.' T. L. Pangle, *The Spirit of Modern Republicanism: The Moral Vision of the American Founders and the philosophy of Locke*, Chicago University Press, Chicago, 1988, p.2
33. J. Tully, *An Approach to Political Philosophy*, p.137
34. J. Locke, *Two Treatises*, p.207
35. Ibid.
36. Ibid., p.224
37. R. H. Cox, *Locke on War and Peace*, p.155
38. J. Locke, *Two Treatises*, p.207
39. Ibid., p.208
40. Ibid., p.209
41. Ibid., p.210
42. Ibid., p.211
43. D. W. Bromley, *Environment and Economy*, Blackwell, Oxford, 1991, pp.7–8

8 Political Philosophy and World History: The Examples of Hegel and Kant

INTRODUCTION

The object of this chapter is threefold. Firstly, the purpose is to look closely at the connection between the intellectual enterprises of political philosophy and the philosophy of history. Secondly, the purpose is to outline and criticize the connection as seen by Kant and Hegel. Thirdly, the purpose is to draw some preliminary conclusions about the advantages and disadvantages of underpinning a political philosophy with a view of history. In drawing these conclusions I should like to explore the belief that although it may be possible to undertake the philosophy of history with little direct regard for political philosophy contrariwise it would be mistaken, if not foolish, to present a political philosophy without taking into account problems raised by the philosophy of history. Finally, I intend to look at the implications of the tying together of political philosophy and the philosophy of history for the study of world politics.

In bringing together these two different enterprises I am conscious that many writers on political philosophy and political theory shy away from the discussion of history. If we take D. D. Raphael's *Problems of Political Philosophy* and N. Barry's *Introduction to Modern Political Theory* as representative examples of contemporary political philosophy then it may fairly be said that historical issues are touched upon only in passing. For Raphael 'social and political philosophy is, of course, a branch of philosophy; it is an application of philosophical thinking to ideas about society and the State. Philosophy has taken many different forms, but I find it useful to interpret the main tradition of western philosophy as having had two connected aims: (a) the clarification of concepts, for the purpose of (b) the critical evaluation of beliefs.'[1] The approach favoured appears to be one firmly anchored in the present with the emphasis strongly placed on seeking to determine the optimal political arrangements for a society. This view is reinforced by

Barry when he says, 'a convenient, albeit necessarily crude, way of approaching some of the problems of political theory is through particular frameworks of analysis: of a methodological rather than an overtly political kind ... In these areas problems of language, meaning, the explanation of social order and substantive normative justification appear together and the activity of political theorising consists very much in elucidating these aspects'.[2] The problems of social order are considered ahistorically. The society concerned is usually seen in the abstract and its structure is outlined from the standpoint of what might be favoured by the rational individual.

Thus the focus of political philosophy is doubly individual. First it is individual because the project is seen through the eyes of a self-conscious person who is capable of moral discrimination. Secondly, it is individual since most political philosophers consider the arrangements of one nation-state taken in isolation. Classical writers like Plato and Aristotle were seeking to outline the best polity and this focus continues to this day in the writings of the most notable political theorists. In his *A Theory of Justice* John Rawls, for example, concerns himself with the rational self and the one good society. 'Thus we are to imagine that those who engage in social cooperation choose together, in one joint act, the principles which are to assign basic rights and duties and to determine the division of social benefits. Men are to decide in advance how they are to regulate their claims against one another and what is to be the foundation charter of their society. Just as each person must decide by rational reflection what constitutes his good, that is, the system of ends which it is rational for him to pursue, so a group of persons must decide once and for all what is to count among them as just and unjust.'[3] For the purposes of analysis the history and external relations of the one good society are set to one side.

In contrast with the usual focus of political philosophy on the impersonal individual the focus of the philosophy of history is generally on the group, the state or collection of states. Much as political philosophy is concerned with the calculation of action, the weighing of possibilities and deliberation on outcomes, the philosophy of history concerns itself with the nature of explanation or, if explanation is too ambitious a word, the nature of interpretation. As R. F. Atkinson puts it, 'philosophers of history, at least those writing recently in English, have mainly been concerned with the significance and truth of historical statements, the possibility of objectivity, with explanation, causation and values'.[4] The stress of political philosophy is on the evaluation of the present and a projection of the future, the emphasis of the philosophy of history is, in contrast, on the evaluation of the past. As we might expect, in terms of time-scale the focus is different.

Political philosophy concerns itself with the unfolding drama of the lives of individuals, world history concerns itself more often with the unfolding drama of the life of the species. Political philosophy tends to move outward from the individual to the group and the world, the philosophy of history generally moves inward from the species to the individual. The study of world politics sits uneasily between the two, perhaps resembling the philosophy of history more in its view of the past and political philosophy more in its view of the future. According to Paul Viotti and Mark Kauppi typical questions for the discipline of international relations are: 'Why do wars occur? Is nationalism the primary cause? Or ideology? Or the lack of world government? Or misperception? Or are people innately aggressive? How can stability be achieved? Why is there such tremendous social and economic inequality between different regions of the world?'[5] The philosophy of history lends itself more easily to a view of individuals as being moved along by events, whereas political philosophy is more adapted to seeing the individual as the initiator of events. My view is that political action becomes more intelligible and effective where there is a confluence of the two views in the standpoint of both the observer and the actor. If Viotti and Kauppi are right about the questions that trouble international relations then the study of world politics stands to gain a great deal if political philosophy and the philosophy of history can be synthesized.

UNIVERSAL HISTORY AND POLITICAL PHILOSOPHY IN KANT

In Kant we find such an attempted synthesis. The best known and probably the most important of Kant's writings on political theory is *Perpetual Peace*. I find it to be a well-argued and persuasive essay which is of great interest in the context of the present post-Cold War era. Kant's suggestions about the progressive nature of republican government, the importance of the separation of powers within states and the role that a continually expanding peaceful federation can play seem timely to me. Kant brings out the positive elements in world society and shows what statesmen can do to further the cause of progress. One of the great levers for progress with Kant is the freedom of expression and the public discussion of political policy. Kant believes that public argument is good provided it is backed up with a respect for rights and an acceptance of sovereign authority.

In the first supplement to this enlightened essay Kant brings together his view of history and his political outlook. Kant is concerned to discover what can guarantee the success of his plan for perpetual peace. He feels that everyone will concur with the wisdom of his plan, but few will see it as applicable in practice because of the shortsightedness of political leaders and subjects. Kant knows that the good sense of the plan will not of itself bring about change.

In Kant's view universal history can be looked at to provide the necessary guarantee of gradual progress towards the goal of lasting peace. 'The guarantee of perpetual peace is nothing less than that great artist nature. In her mechanical course we see that her aim is to produce a harmony among men, against their will and indeed through their discord. As a necessity working to laws we do not know, we call it fate. But, considering its design in world history, we call it providence inasmuch as we discern in it the profound wisdom of a higher cause which predetermines the course of nature and directs it to the objective final end of the human race.'[6] Kant sees world history as the work of nature and providence. Kant's assumption is that individuals as historical beings are not wholly in charge of their own destinies. This is because we are both phenomenal and noumenal beings. As well as having a foot in the rational intellectual realm, human beings also have a foot in nature. As phenomenal beings we can be regarded as conditioned and subject to external forces, whereas as noumenal beings we can regard ourselves as potentially self-determining and able to act according to principle.

In so far as we can be seen as phenomenal beings and subject to nature we can be regarded as conditioned by mechanistic laws. In society the effect of such mechanistic laws are necessarily large-scale, such as the incidence of marriages and deaths. Individuals may regard such activities as subject to variation according to their own tastes and practices (particularly with regard to the first!), yet this does not prevent them from being subject to aggregate effects. We are as much driven by circumstances as we are in turn able to condition them.

Now Kant believes that such mechanistic effects on a global scale will lead to the necessity for world peace. In the first place he thinks that geographical or ecological pressures will lead eventually to a need for peoples to cooperate. The expansion of populations will ultimately mean that all inhabitable parts of the globe will be settled and exploited. When the room for outward expansion has disappeared Kant thinks states and individuals will have to concentrate upon the better exploitation of the resources at their command. We can see this kind of pressure operating in today's world where issues such as global warming and industrial contamination become concerns for all nations.

In the second place Kant thinks that economic forces will lead to a greater integration of states. Commerce and trade flourish best under peaceful conditions. It is in the ultimate interest of each state to encourage the widest possible exchange of goods and skills. No state can be wholly self-sufficient.

The desire of the former Soviet Union to cooperate with the G7 group of advanced industrial nations demonstrated the relevance of this point. Even the Unites States is not entirely free to act contrary to the interests of the other advanced states of the world.

Finally, Kant believes that military and political pressures will lead to the same need for greater cooperation and respect for international law. 'As nature saw to it that men could live everywhere in the world, she also despotically willed that they should do so, even against their inclination and without this ought being based on a concept of duty to which they were bound by a moral law. She chose war as the means to this end.'[7] Kant believes that war will ultimately destroy itself. The ferocity and destructiveness with which wars are fought will increase to such an extent that no state with an educated citizenry will contemplate its possibility. For Kant war itself is the greatest antidote to war. Once political leaders realize that they must conduct their affairs without resort to war then this will have the effect of moralizing their policies. Since war is a means of resolving international disputes without reference to a set of rules or arbitration its increasing infrequency will oblige political leaders to deal more justly with one another.

Kant's view is that injustice in the end undermines itself. The process of world history will ensure that the immoral wiles of unscrupulous political leaders are defeated. The outcomes of world politics and the aims of good political leadership ultimately coalesce. Morality and prudence do not in the long term conflict with one another. 'Moral evil has the inescapable property of being opposed to and destructive of its own purposes (especially in the relationships between evil men); thus it gives place to the moral principle of the good, though only through a slow progress.'[8] This belief underpins the success of Kant's political philosophy. For if it could be shown that political leaders can consistently flourish without paying heed to morality then the motivation for progressive change is undermined.

Kant is extremely vulnerable to criticism on this point. He says in his defence: 'The tutelary divinity of morality yields not to Jupiter, for this tutelary divinity of force still is subject to fate. That is, reason is not yet sufficiently enlightened to survey the entire series of predetermining causes, and such vision would be necessary for one to be able to foresee with certainty the happy or unhappy effects which follow human actions by the mechanism of nature (though we know enough to have hope that they will accord with our wishes)'.[9] Kant's view is that we can never know enough about the process or human society and world history to predict with certainty the outcome of present policies and events. The prudential political leader who tries to act with only expediency in mind, and so with an eye only to present success will have no absolutely clear indication as to which policy and present actions will bring success. In being solely expedient political leaders will therefore place themselves in the hands of fate (which for Kant is symbolized by the god Jupiter). In other words, expedient policies may have entirely the opposite effect. They may turn out to be inexpedient. Kant's way out of this dilemma is to recommend that the politician cease trying to be solely prudent and try to combine prudence with morality. This the politician can do by taking a progressive view of history. Politicians should, in short, avail themselves of the guarantee of progress Kant finds in the philosophy of history.

I find this view that world history viewed philosophically can provide a guarantee of progress a bit disappointing. We might see it as particularly disappointing in the light of the highly voluntarist quality of Kant's ethics. In his ethics Kant will not countenance the possibility that free action may not be possible. Ethical action depends, in his view, on our rising above circumstances and instinct. But for progress to come about in politics circumstances and instinct have apparently to prevail. Taken at face value this assertion might justifiably be seen as complacent and even dangerous.

If such an interpretation is correct Kant seems to fall a good deal behind the historical view taken by Machiavelli. Machiavelli argues we can take advantage of the opportunities offered to us by fortune through virtuous intervention. Machiavelli estimates (perhaps generously) that we have a 50 per cent chance of altering the course of events. For approximately the other 50 per cent we are in the hands of fate. 'Because free choice cannot be ruled out, I believe that it is probably true that fortune is the arbiter of half the things we do, leaving the other half or so to be controlled by ourselves.'[10] Kant seems to suggest, in contrast, that good political leaders can affect events but nature is necessary to provide an assurance for the ultimate success of their efforts. We have to rely on providence to see us home. This is a precarious aspect of Kant's political philosophy, thoroughly compounded in Hegel's notion of world history driven by spirit. In this vision we become nothing more than passengers in an apparently unstoppable vehicle. No doubt circumstances can force changes in the behaviour of people, but Kant's own political/moral perspective seems to imply that change would come best from within. Such internal, motivational changes depends upon enlightenment and individual commitment. The idea that such a process of internal education can be accelerated or even avoided by the march of world history leaves a great deal to chance.

The difficulty with Kant (and Hegel also in this respect) is that the past or the realm of world history is not seen as a political realm where successes may have been achieved and mistakes made. In his analysis of history Kant follows the example of many a historian by removing the notion of the causality of the will. Kant's teleological account of world history does not see individuals as responsible for their own fate. Individuals in history are subject to forces beyond their control. Thus, whilst Kant's moral philosophy does full honour to human dignity, the philosophy of history sells it short. As a consequence a hiatus tends to develop between politicians as moral actors and politicians as historical actors. As historical actors they are at the mercy of forces beyond their control, but as moral actors they must see themselves as being able to shape events.

Despland in *Kant on History and Religion* has a very plausible defence of Kant's position. He argues, as I have previously in *Kant's Political Philosophy*,[11] that the main status of Kant's progressive view of history is that of a moral incentive to individuals in the political realm. 'Thus Kant's faith in Nature and Culture is a faith in the possibility of a progressive humanization of man and realization of his freedom through wise social arrangements and historic achievements. It stands opposed equally to the conservatism that sees no possible moral benefits in political reform and to the utopianism that sees no possible moral benefits made available through the political arrangements history has bequeathed to us.'[12] Just as in the *Critique of Practical Reason* the notion of God is put forward not as a factual claim about the world but rather as an incentive for us to seek the highest good in human life, so the notion of the natural progress of mankind to a better world is put forward as an aid to the moral politician. It is the moral politician's ultimate insurance that his actions are not in vain.

This argument is most justifiable in terms of Kant's philosophy as a whole which gives precedence to practical reason over theoretical reason. For Kant our knowledge of the world is always unsure and constantly subject to revision because we ourselves supply many of the means (through our cognitive faculties) of knowing. Practical reason in contrast has far greater reality, since in the will we have an object which corresponds with its nature. Thus if a moral politician wishes to present as the maxim of his actions the notion of a peaceful world community, this notion can attain in his actions far greater objectivity than any theory about the nature of history. Kant's conception of necessary progress redeems itself possibly as a guide to present action. 'In this manner nature guarantees perpetual peace by the mechanism of human passions. Certainly she does not do so with sufficient certainty for us to predict the future in any theoretical sense, but adequately from a practical point of view, making it our duty to work toward this end, which is not just a chimerical one.'[13] But is this standpoint which combines moral assuredness with factual scepticism satisfactory?

In an interesting book on *Kantian Ethics and Socialism*, many of whose perspectives are persuasive, Harry van der Linden suggests that there are four major deficiencies to Kant's philosophy of history. First, van der Linden believes that Kant 'overestimates the scope of the cunning of nature as a medium of progress'.[14] This is a point that I have already made. Kant expects too much of a process that he himself is somewhat sceptical about. It seems that we can expect some help from the course of human events towards the realization of our ideals, but we cannot place reliance on fortune. We cannot make progress entirely a matter of good or bad luck. Secondly, and this follows from van der Linden's initial point, 'more emphasis must be placed upon moral action as a vehicle of progress'.[15] I would concur with this view but it must be realized that it leads to an alteration to Kant's primarily passive view of history. If more is to depend on what we the participants in human history and society do then more scope has to be given for our effectiveness. Kant appears to limit our impact on society to individual actions and the actions of statesmen. Some role should also be found, I think, for institutions and collectivities in the vision of progress, however unreliable they might be.

This conclusion ties in with van der Linden's third point, namely, that 'politics need not be the main instrument of progress'.[16] Kant's stress on the moral politician in the process of bringing about improvement tends to overlook the role that other actors may play. Corporations, classes, political parties and trade unions are all examples of social movements that can help in the implementation of change. I think it would be a mistake to assume that such organizations are the only means whereby change can be brought about, but we can expect more than what Kant seems to suggest by his silence on the issue. This brings us to van der Linden's fourth point that 'the ultimate aim of history should not be a mere ideational union of good wills'.[17] Here I agree with van der Linden that it is helpful to be more concrete than Kant in specifying how individuals are to live in harmony with one another. The notions of a kingdom of ends and an ethical commonwealth which appear in Kant's moral reasoning might now benefit from being spelled out in greater detail. In this respect contemporary political philosophy stands out from Kant's interpretation concerned as it is with the grounds for coercion and the outlawing of resistance. Writers like Rawls and Habermas provide a great deal more detail as to what would be the ideal state of affairs.

Kant's treatment of the philosophy of history and political philosophy and their connection is innovative and provocative but he also leaves a large number of gaps in terms of agency and opportunities. For me it is not too attractive just to wait for chance to allow a moral politician to emerge. Equally, Kant so restricts the opportunities for lawful and ethical opposition that the postulate of progress for the ordinary citizen might seem of mainly fictional value.

WORLD HISTORY AND POLITICAL PHILOSOPHY IN HEGEL

If, as Kain points out (in his interesting article, 'Kant's Political Theory and Philosophy of History'),[18] the merit of Kant's approach to political theory is to bring together politics and world history, Hegel's approach can be seen as a regression to a previous level. For Hegel decisively separates political philosophy and world history. Political philosophy is confined to a sphere in which world history plays little part. World history, in contrast, occurs on a much grander and more tragic scale beyond the day-to-day concerns of political leaders and ordinary citizens. 'Without rhetorical exaggeration, a simply truthful combination of the miseries that have overwhelmed the noblest of nations and politics, and the finest exemplars of private virtue – forms a picture of most fearful aspect, and excites emotions of the profoundest and most hopeless sadness, counterbalanced by no consolatory result. We endure in beholding it a mental torture, allowing no defence or escape but the consideration that what has happened could not be otherwise; that it is a fatality which no intervention could alter.'[19]

Hegel's attitude to world history and political philosophy is made clear in his *Philosophy of Right*. The purpose of political philosophy is to promote acceptance in the mind of the enquiring citizen of the here and now. 'To comprehend what is, this is the task of philosophy, because what is, is reason. Whatever happens every individual is a child of his time; so philosophy too is its own time apprehended in thoughts. It is just as absurd to fancy that a philosophy can transcend its contemporary world as it is to fancy that an individual can overleap his own age, jump over Rhodes. If his theory really goes beyond the world as it is and builds an ideal one as it ought to be, that world exists indeed, but only in his opinions, an unsubstantial element where anything you please may in fancy be built.'[20] In an Aristotelian fashion Hegel argues that existing institutions necessarily perform rational functions. In their construction institutions bear upon them the impact of the intellect. This intellectual element (Hegel is unclear about its origin) in the make-up of institutions has to be brought out by political philosophy in order for it to be appreciated by the citizen.

As we have seen in Chapter 3, Hegel's approach to political philosophy is non-activist. He does not see himself as advocating a certain set of institutions which concerned citizens should strive to bring into being. In this respect his approach is contrary to that found in contemporary political philosophy, particularly of the liberal school. Unlike Rawls or Nozick who have little difficulty about suggesting how they think a society should be best ordered,[21] Hegel believes he has no distinct kind of programme to advocate. As he sees it, the programme already exists within the society. The political philosopher ought not to try to impose an extra programme upon the existing one. Hegel does not want citizens to shape their environment, rather he wants them to come to terms better with their existing one.

Hegel's political philosophy seems to me to be a curious one for a dialectical philosopher to present. The dialectical method, we might plausibly argue, leads to a view of things in the full flow of their movement. It might seem that the use of such a method would catch individuals both in their process of coming to be and ceasing to be. Indeed, on one view, the central category in Hegel's own *Science of Logic* is becoming.[22] Being is not just the median term between being and non-being, it is their truth. Yet there seems little stress on such a process of becoming in Hegel's political philosophy. Instead of institutions being viewed as in a process of change they are seen as already complete and finished. Instead of an account of society and politics as becoming, we get in many respects an account of a society that has already come.

In Hegel's defence it might justly be said that he does not ignore the dialectical method in the *Philosophy of Right*. The institutions of civil society and the state are dialectically derived from the basic supposition of the free will. Many of the transitions are of a convincingly dialectical kind, especially the transition from the family to civil society. Hegel does persuasively show how civil society comes on the scene as a second home for the individual. But the dialectical process of deduction cannot disguise the fact that Hegel is attempting to present the political system of the day as something finished and complete. The question of the further development of domestic and world politics is relegated to a peripheral issue.

There are very many sound political reasons for this apparent timidity in Hegel's approach to political philosophy. Hegel experienced the French Revolution and this led to great doubts in his mind about the value of radical political change. Hegel possibly felt that a programmatic political philosophy invites citizens too readily to take a step in the dark. With Burke, Hegel may well have thought that sound political action conserves at the same time as it might seek to change. As Burke puts it, 'a state without the means of some change is without the means of its conservation. Without such means it might even risque the loss of that part of the constitution which it wished most religiously to preserve.'[23] Above all, Hegel may have had a reverence for the impersonal rule of law in the face of extreme democratic demands for the participation of all in the making of law. With Kant Hegel had severe doubts as to whether the people could rule themselves. More than possibly, after the experiences of the French Revolution, Hegel feared anarchy. Hegel believed that society's rulers should listen to the voice of public opinion, but not follow it.[24] In his opinion the people did not rightly know what they wanted. We might in contrast think the people often do know what they want, but quite often they are not consistent in what they want. This leads to a process of intepretation on the part of those in authority which might not be the same thing as Hegel's apparent total disregard of popular pressure, but nonetheless channels and redirects the popular voice. In this way it may be possible to govern as effectively as Hegel would wish without depriving the public of a voice.

So Hegel's political philosophy is non-participatory and generally conservative. At its darkest his political philosophy preaches resignation before the facts of the present. And so all the decisive action is passed over into the realm of the philosophy of history, as this passage indicates:

> 'Justice and virtue, wrongdoing, power and vice, talents and their achievements, passions strong and weak, guilt and innocence, grandeur in individual and national life, autonomy, fortune and misfortune of states and individuals, all these have their specific significance and worth in the field of known actuality; therein they are judged and therein they have their partial, though only partial justification. World-history, however, is above the point of view from which these things matter.'[25]

With Hegel world history sweeps out of the way the issues of contemporary political philosophy. Present citizens may appear to become mere grist to the mill of historical development. Indeed Hegel conjures up a vision of world history which is somewhat akin to a hurricane destroying everything in its path.

Just as Kant sees history and world politics as leading to consequences unwilled by any of the participants so Hegel thinks that there may operate in history a similar force which he calls the cunning of reason (*List der Vernunft*). This cunning of reason 'sets the passions to work for itself, while that which develops its existence through such impulsion pays the penalty and suffers loss'.[26] In working itself out an idea of the cunning of reason may have to sacrifice and abandon the individual. Hegel sees this not as a fault of the convoluted development of the cunning of reason but as the outcome of the limitations of individuals. History may well go through some regretful periods as a consequence of the envy, greed and ambition of certain individuals. But history takes its own revenge. So grandiose are the purposes of history it is possible for Hegel to say 'that as a general rule, individuals come under the category of means to an ulterior end'.[27]

Where world history and contemporary politics appear to meet with Hegel is in the state. The state embodies one of the aims of world history. Freedom – which Hegel sees as the final goal of history – is only possible within the modern Germanic state. Thus those who act to foster the state at the same time do the work of world spirit. But from the perspective of world history Hegel makes this extremely difficult for the individual. Since in many respects this standpoint of world history is above that of ordinary law or ethics, the individual who is to promote progress may be called upon to act in conflict with the laws of his actual state.

The great difficulty then with the manner in which Hegel relates political philosophy to world history is that it leads to a dangerous hiatus between present and past action. The separation of political philosophy from world history leaves the individual political leader with no overall responsibility for future developments and the philosopher of history, understandably, takes no responsibility for present events.

Moreover, Hegel provides unjustified reassurances at both levels. In political philosophy his disregard for world history leads (at least within the state) to a resignation before present political realities. At the level of world history, because the politics of the present are set to one side, an unfounded optimism reigns about the course of the world. World spirit marches relentlessly onward towards freedom, regardless of what present minor difficulties we may encounter. This is optimism of the most breathtaking kind.

In his political philosophy Hegel, I believe, makes too strong a case for contemporary inaction on the part of citizens. Politicians simply modify existing laws, reinforce the authority of the monarch and encourage citizens to remain in their private spheres. Citizens are allowed to voice their opinions, but if they are to have an impact they have to fit in with the current arrangement of society. According to Hegel, individuals are set in their ways and if there is an imprint of ethicality in their present pattern of life this should be encouraged. Hegel is all in favour of the unselfconscious citizen who observes unquestioningly the laws and customs of his land. From such a viewpoint the notion of making the future is too large a goal to be consciously contemplated. Hegel's valuable suggestions about present reform in his political philosophy pale into insignificance when compared with the scope given to the cunning of reason in history.

CONCLUSION

I argue for a more participatory view of world history and political philosophy than Hegel suggests. In politics active citizenship can, I think, bring out and safeguard the positive features of a society. Active citizenship need not necessarily manifest itself as dissidence. Indeed, the positive features which Hegel himself is fond of: such as a well-ordered civil society which channels competiveness, and a civil service which engenders competence within itself and the wider society, might well be better advanced by active citizenship rather than unselfconscious obedience. The kind of passivity Hegel favours might well in the long-run prejudice such features.

In terms of world history it would be desirable if each individual, as Marcuse suggests, became aware of themselves as part of a *project* and saw their roles in terms of the wider development of society. In Marcuse's view, 'the way in which a society organizes the life of its members involves an initial choice between historical alternatives which are determined by the inherited level of culture. The choice itself results from the play of the dominant interests. It anticipates specific modes of transforming and utilizing man and nature and rejects other modes. It is one "project" of realization among others.'[28] Each society is already engaged upon a project so there is no way of avoiding the question of our allegiance. No doubt, it is not every individual who plays a significant role in history, but each individual is the carrier of historical traditions and goals. This process of transmission can be done well or badly. By being more conscious of the options open to themselves citizens can play a greater part in making their collective future. Because if we set to one side Kant's notion of providence and Hegel's notion of world spirit, it seems an inescapable conclusion for us to draw that, despite all appearances to the contrary, individuals and individuals in groups make their own future.

I have to accept that Hegel's philosophy of history adds excitement to our picture of life. From the observer's standpoint it genuinely is gripping stuff. His conflictual account gives an insight into the dynamic of history. We move from one condition of imperfection to the next. Each stage though represents, we are encouraged to believe, a new and more advanced realization of freedom. But this though leaves his political philosophy looking something like an anticlimax. It seems that nothing on a world historical scale can happen now. All the action is taken care of by world spirit. Today's individuals are left only to mark time for the next surge of events.

It would be untrue to say that Hegel's political philosophy ignores world history since respect is shown to the present as a product of world history. But no respect is shown to present individuals as creators of the future. Hegel appears to fear present action. In his political philosophy academic integrity and insight is preserved at the expense of present and future experimentation and innovation.

With Hegel it seems that one has to forget the philosophy of history to do political philosophy and, vice versa, you have to forget political philosophy to do philosophical history. For most of the time political philosophy and the philosophy of history move in contradictory directions. Where they meet in the present they do so only to bring an arbitrary halt to each other's activities.

In my view, this won't do at all. We need a philosophy of history that opens up the perspectives of political philosophy and a political philosophy which capitalizes on the processes of world history. The subject of political philosophy should be the individual as a historical being, and the subject of the philosophy of history should be a diverse and self-creating mankind. Kant gets much nearer this vision than Hegel, though Hegel has a greater insight into the potential grandeur of the project.

NOTES

1. D. D. Raphael, *Problems of Political Philosophy*, Macmillan, London, 1990, pp.7–8
2. N. P. Barry, *An Introduction to Modern Political Theory*, Macmillan, London, 1987, p.16
3. J. Rawls, *A Theory of Justice*, Oxford University Press, Oxford, 1972, pp.11–12
4. R. F. Atkinson, *Knowledge and Explanation in History*, Macmillan, London, 1978, p.4
5. P. R. Viotti and M. V. Kauppi, *International Relations Theory*, Maxwell Macmillan International, New York, 1990, p.1
6. I. Kant, *Perpetual Peace* in *Kant: Selections*, ed. L.W. Beck, Macmillan, London, 1988, p.440; *Akademische Ausgabe*, VIII, p.362
7. I. Kant, *Kant: Selections*, p.442; *Akademische Ausgabe*, p.364
8. I. Kant, *Kant: Selections*, p.452; *Akademische Ausgabe*, p.379
9. I. Kant, *Kant: Selections*, pp.446–7; *Akademische Ausgabe*, p.370
10. N. Machiavelli, *The Prince*, Penguin, Harmondsworth, 1968, p.130
11. H. Williams, *Kant's Political Philosophy*, Blackwell, Oxford, 1983, p.244
12. M. Despland, *Kant on History and Religion*, McGill/Queen's University Press, Montreal and London, 1973, p.88
13. I. Kant, *Kant: Selections*, p.445; *Akademische Ausgabe*, p.368
14. H. van der Linden, *Kantian Ethics and Socialism*, Hackett, Indianapolis & London, 1988, p.191
15. Ibid.
16. Ibid.
17. Ibid.
18. P. Kain, 'Kant's Political Theory and Philosophy of History', *Clio*, 18, 1989, pp.325–45

19. G. W. F. Hegel, *Philosophy of History*, Dover, New York, 1956, p.21
20. G. W. F. Hegel, *Philosophy of Right*, Oxford University Press, Oxford, 1969, p.11
21. R. Nozick, *Anarchy, State and Utopia*, Blackwell, Oxford, 1974, pp.ix
22. G. W. F. Hegel, *Science of Logic*, Allen & Unwin, London, 1969, pp.105–6. Cf. H. Williams, *Hegel, Heraclitus and Marx's Dialectic*, Harvester, Hemel Hempstead, 1989, p.119
23. E. Burke, *Reflections on the French Revolution*, Penguin, Harmondsworth, 1973, p.106
24. G. W. F. Hegel, *Philosophy of Right*, para. 317, p.204
25. Ibid., para. 345, p.217
26. G. W. F. Hegel, *Philosophy of History*, p.33
27. Ibid.
28. H. Marcuse, *One Dimensional Man*, Sphere Books, London, 1968, p.14

9 Justice in One Country?

TWO TYPES OF JUSTICE

By the term justice in this chapter I shall mean both legal justice and distributive justice. Legal justice refers to the existence of law and its implementation by a publicly recognized set of institutions like law courts and the police. Distributive justice refers to a quite wider sphere, namely the set of arrangements a society may have which ensures a publicly accepted fair allocation of resources and job positions. The two meanings of justice are not unconnected but questions of distributive justice tend now to arouse the greater controversy in political philosophy. Whereas most contemporary western political philosophers agree that some mechanism to ensure the effectiveness of procedural justice is necessary in a society,[1] many dispute that a means has to be found to ensure that some form of distributive justice is attained. The philosophy of the new right in particular focuses on demonstrating that attempts at redistributing income and wealth through the state are likely to have deleterious rather than positive effects.

There is a widely shared view (and possibly justifiably) that the socialist experiment which took place in the Soviet Union and its dependent states throughout a major part of this century represents a mistaken turn in human history. The idea of a fully socialized economy running according to a centrally formulated plan seems in practice to have failed. This represented one vast undertaking aimed at creating an ideal system of distributive justice. If this is hesitatingly, perhaps, generally agreed, there is probably more widespread agreement that one part of this experiment was a complete and utter failure. An aspect of the experiment that few, even on the left, would seek to defend is the attempt by Stalin to create 'socialism in one country'.

What I want to suggest here is that the attempts to create a new system of justice in Russia and Eastern Europe after the fall of communism have gone in two contradictory directions. The major change, which is visible for all to see, is that the leaders of those countries have given up any attempt at bringing about a satisfactory system of distributive justice solely within the domestic context by relying upon the distributive and re-distributive efforts of a state bureaucracy. However, a second direction which change has taken, which is perhaps less visible but probably just as significant, is that state leaders have come to believe that the best way in which to achieve legal justice is to centre the loyalty of their peoples upon the national or ethnic community.

The change towards a different concept of distributive justice has implied the integration of the ex-Soviet bloc into wider world society, but the second change carries with it not the promise of integration but rather the threat of disintegration and fragmentation.

Within socialist circles themselves there were always considerable doubts about the wisdom of the strategy of autarkic development. It was not a strategy which was in the mind of many Bolshevik leaders in 1917. And, if we are to believe Lenin's words in his pamphlets of the time, his strategy was entirely the opposite one of linking up Russia with socialist change in the rest of the world. The object of many of the Bolsheviks was a dramatic and immensely ambitious world revolution. Lenin's pamphlet on *Imperialism* was written very much in this vein.[2] In common with most Marxists Lenin had believed before 1916 that Russia would have to go through a two-stage revolution leading from its feudal condition at the turn of the century through a bourgeois period to a higher socialist stage in the more distant future. However, Lenin's reading of the First World War as an inter-imperialist struggle of global proportions led him to the conclusion that local, national revolutions were no longer possible in the European context. Each domestic upheaval in Europe would have worldwide implications. According to Lenin, 'capitalism has now singled out a handful (less than one tenth of the individuals on the globe; less than one-fifth at a most generous and liberal calculation) of exceptionally rich and powerful states which plunder the whole world simply by "clipping coupons"'.[3] The combination of the power of finance capital wielded by the banks and the power of monopoly held by industrial capitalists had led to an aggressive organization of the leading bourgeois countries, vying with each other for influence and control. The struggle amongst finance capitalists was a struggle for world domination. This period of imperialism was characterized for Lenin by the export of capital. Whereas in its competitive stage the capitalist centre had colonized the periphery primarily to acquire raw materials and create new markets, in its monopoly stage the capitalist centre was exploiting the periphery as an outlet for surplus capital. Lenin's conclusion is emphatic. 'Imperialism is the eve of the social revolution of the proletariat. This has been confirmed since 1917 on a world-wide scale.'[4]

Within capitalist circles the autarkic path of development was always regarded as a mistake. Liberal political economists have very many sensible lines of criticism which show the weaknesses and deficiencies which follow from isolation from the world economy. One of the worst dangers is possibly ineffeciency. The lack of competition from businesses and merchants from other states leads to complacency in the production and finishing of goods. Isolation can lead to nobody getting what they want when they want it. Quality is poor because people are not able to buy the best that is available, and some goods are not available at all because the autarkic state is unable to produce it. Exposure to the world economy brings with it greater risks, but also greater potential rewards. It is not surprising that socialism in one country failed given the inquisitiveness, restlessness and infinite desires of human individuals. Economic autarky was not the sole reason that state socialism failed in Russia and its satellite states but it was a key reason.

One of the most marked features of the changes in Eastern European countries since 1989 has been their readiness to embrace an openness in their economic dealings with the rest of the world. Not surprisingly these countries want to enjoy the fruits of capitalist development, particularly what is best in the capitalist mode. States, regions and cities in Eastern Europe are falling over themselves to estabish economic links with the west and rest of the developed world. This (probably quite rightly) is seen as the path to economic prosperity.

With the final collapse of Marxist-Leninist hegemony in the Eastern European states those states are seeking not only new economic forms but also new forms of political legitimacy adapted to the new age. In this second, political, respect the cause of internationalism seems not to have fared as well. In contrast to economic openness there seems to be developing a political desire to go it alone. The thinking seems to be that although economic prosperity has to be built on an international basis, justice – both legal and distributive justice – has to be established nationally or locally. Each nation or ethnic group appears to believe that it has to look to itself alone to found legal justice and social fairness.

MARXIAN JUSTICE

I want here to look at the possible philosophical justification for this line of development in the idea of justice the Russian and Eastern Europe context and its likely criticisms. The discussion of justice is deeply rooted in political philosophy and it is an important theme of contemporary liberal political thought. Justice forms the topic of the first major book in history of political thought, Plato's *Republic*. Interestingly Plato runs procedural justice and distributive justice together in his account of the just state. It might even be argued that Plato eliminates legal justice in devising his perfect system of distributive justice. Essentially, justice hangs upon the philosophical insight of the ruling Guardian class. Members of this group recognize that justice is to be attained by specialization or a proper division of labour, in particular a division of labour between ruler and ruled.[5] In contrast, contemporary liberal political philosophy has given a great deal of emphasis to distributive justice as distinct from purely legal justice. Thinkers like John Rawls tend to take it for granted that individuals will accept the legal authority of the state over them and devote their attention to the kind of practices, institutions and economic arrangements that such individuals will find acceptable. Rawls's emphasis is on justice as fairness rather than justice as a means of maintaining the peace.

In contrast to the general tradition of political thought the question of justice has only been sparsely dealt with in the Marxist canon. On the whole, Marxist scholarship has not dealt with the idea of justice separately from other political concepts. Generally justice within this view is seen as dependent on the wider economic development of society. Marx himself has a radical, utopian critique of justice which has generally set the agenda for the subsequent treatment of the topic by communist thinkers. Allen Buchanan (1982) argues that there are five aspects to this radical critique of justice:

1. One of the most serious indictments of capitalism – and of all class-divided societies – is not that they are unjust or that they violate persons' rights, but that they are based upon defective modes of production which make reliance upon conceptions of justice and right necessary.
2. The demands of justice cannot be satisfied in the circumstances which make conceptions of justice necessary; thus efforts to achieve justice inevitably fail.
3. Conceptions of rights or justice will not play a major motivational role in the revolutionary struggle to replace capitalism with communism.
4. Communism will be a society in which juridical concepts – including the juridical concept of respect – have no significant role in structuring social relations.
5. The concept of a person as essentially a being with a sense of justice and who is a bearer of rights is a radically defective concept that could only arise in a radically defective form of human society.[6]

Justice with Marx forms part of the superstructure of a society which is transformed as the economic basis of society revolutionizes itself. In part justice is marginal in the Marxist tradition because it is a radical theory of distributive justice in which the proletariat is seen as taking command of its own fate and allocating positions and rewards according to its own criterion of equality, and in part it is marginal because in such a cataclysmic view of society it seems churlish to raise questions of legitimacy. With Marx, as with Plato, the question of legal justice is submerged by the all-embracing concern to establish an acceptable system of distributive justice.

Marx's view of justice is deliberately utopian. He is aiming at a society where relations among individuals have reached such a high level, both materially and culturally, that there is no need for a formal policing of arrangements among people. In other words, he is assuming the Kantian model of social relations, where individuals will never treat each other solely as means but always also as ends, will have been already realized. Marx also makes the further assumption that the principal cause which prevents such a society from being achieved immediately is the peculiar economic arrangements of a capitalist society. This is a useful hypothesis – a hypothesis which we should not discard altogether – in measuring the standard of progress of a society, however, it is a hypothesis which is not suited to depicting free individuals who will always have the choice whether or not to do the right thing or, indeed, may wish to dispute what the right thing is in any particular instance. Under some circumstances solidarity may supersede justice as the foundation of a relationship, but we would be unwise to assume from this that we can dispense with justice even within a relationship of solidarity.

In marginalizing questions of justice (particularly of the legal kind) Marxism was, in my view, incorrect. One of the lessons of the ill-fated attempts to implement Marxism appears to be that the *right* has to take precedence over the *good*. Of course, Marxists had to learn this lesson the hard way because they did not pay sufficient attention to political philosophy in the first place. Most of the foundational literature upon the state in the modern period from Hobbes to Kant stresses the importance of first creating a stable political order before going on to discuss issues of distributive justice. The general view was that without order there could be no wealth to distribute. Hobbes is a particularly strong representative of this view, but Kant is equally firm on the issue. As they see it, issues of the fair distribution of the products of human labour do not arise until there is a public legal order which can safeguard property (however unequally held). Locke differs in that he argues that property exists prior to the establishment of civil society and the state, but this is a natural right of acquisition and use, not of exchange and storage. Locke goes on to discuss the rightful exchange and storage of property only after ensuring the public mechanisms to safeguard it and facilitate its transfer are in place.[7] What the priority of the right over the good means in this context is we have first to establish the capacity to maintain and follow rules amongst individuals before we can determine the precise quality of those rules. The serviceability and effectiveness of publicly enforced rules will of course be affected by their quality, but poor quality cannot provide a justification for refusing to accept any kind of system of public legal justice.

THE CLAIMS OF NATIONALISM

'The natural state of man is society'.[8] Herder

Nationalists, in general, claim that state boundaries should correspond with ethnic and customary boundaries. In particular, nationalists are fond of claiming that the boundaries of their state should be the same as that of the ethnic or cultural group of which *they* are part. Many nationalists believe that this is a doctrine that should be universally applied. In other words, they believe that their ethnically founded state should be no more than part of the established pattern of civilized society. Some nationalists are, however, exclusive and concern themselves solely with the cultural and ethnic homogeneity of their own state. The doctrine of this kind of nationalist is often accompanied by the claim of ethnic, racial or cultural superiority. There appear to be no hard and fast rules which distinguish the two types of doctrine. They often merge imperceptibly into one another.

I want here to look briefly at two representative nationalist thinkers. They are two liberal nationalist thinkers, Herder and Mazzini. As liberal nationalists they are drawn to the less exclusive style of nationalism. Their brand of nationalism is compatible with a mild internationalism. Both Herder and Mazzini make claims for the independence of the nations to which they belong which they wish other nations to share. In my view their ideas embody the more attractive aspects of nationalist thinking and might therefore be deemed most appropriate for current European and global circumstances and debate.

Herder's nationalism is based upon a distinctive view of language. In an essay entitled 'On the Origin of Language' submitted to the Royal Prussian Academy of Sciences in 1770 and which received the prize award, Herder argues that it is within a linguistic community that individuals first develop their personalities. Herder argues that 'no man lives for himself alone; he is only one link in the chain of generations, one cipher in the cumulative progression of his species'.[9] As Herder sees it, the human individual is an infinitely sociable being who is dependent upon others in order to advance and progress. Herder sees no clearer illustration of the dependence of the human being upon others than at the moment of birth. This dependency also applies to the child's subsequent infancy. The first steps of the human individual are not taken unaided on immediately entering the world. These first steps are taken only later with the encouragement and support of parents and elders. According to Herder, it is the combined powers of the human species that give to the individual strength and independence. The human being 'comes into the world the weakest and most helpless of all animals'.[10]

For Herder language has its origins in our desire to communicate our experiences to others. Language has its basis in the senses, in what we see, hear, taste, smell and feel. However, it is in our reflection on our feelings and senses that language develops. We communicate in order to survive and prosper, and it is through the family that this communication first takes place. 'Parents accumulate experience not just for themselves but also in order to communicate their share of ideas to the offspring.'[11] Children are better able to survive through having the accumulated experience of their parents communicated to them. For Herder this represents the beginning of community. By means of language, he says, 'the infant is able to enter into communion with the way of thinking and feeling of his progenitors, to take part, as it were, in the workings of the ancestral mind'.[12] The individual's existence is made more secure and enriched through the process of the acquisition of language. As Herder sees it, the bond between individuals and their first language is always an emotional one and consequently 'we associate the strongest sentiments with our native language'.[13] Through language a sense of identity with our family and our wider kin is forged which can persist throughout life. For Herder it is only natural that this link with our kin and community should form the basis of the nation to which we show our allegiance.

Herder puts this sense of identity in highly romantic terms: 'What a treasure language is when kinship groups grow into tribes and nations. Even the smallest of nations in any part of the globe, no matter how undeveloped it may be, cherishes in and through it language the history, poetry, and songs about the great deeds of its forefathers. The language is its collective treasure, the source of its social wisdom and communal self-respect.'[14] Here emotion provides not only the affective basis of the nation but lays the claim to be its overriding purpose. There is no mention of either form of justice, either legal or distributive, as providing a foundation for national identity.

But Herder's views on language seem not to lead him to stridently nationalistic conclusions. For Herder, the development of languages and nations has a progressive logic of its own. We cannot impose on the world an order which it will not accept. Rather we should encourage the development of a different order in which the ties of language are respected: 'It is nature which educates families: the most natural state is, therefore, one nation, an extended family with one national character. This it retains for ages and develops most naturally if the leaders come from the people and are wholly dedicated to it. For a nation is as natural a plant as a family, only with more branches.'[15]

Here it is interesting to see the naturalist argument, employed by thinkers like Grotius and Locke to argue for a universal society of individuals, being employed to argue the opposite. For Herder the natural ties of the human individual are particularist rather than cosmopolitan. In place of the universal sociability of Grotius, Herder puts forward the partial and selective sociability of the human race. Our sociability expresses itself more as a desire to be with others of our own group rather than as a desire to be with others in general.

Herder is, as a consequence, against the multilingual, multinational dynasties of his day such as the Austro-Hungarian empire. He thinks they are artificial formations which will crumble with time as the natural order asserts itself. A natural order is not necessarily a more primitive one, rather it is one where individuals play a role in their own government. As Herder sees it, representation and the recognition of diversity among nations will solve the most pressing of the world's political problems. As individuals and nations progress the liberal nationalist order which nature intended will assert itself.

The Italian nationalist, Mazzini, shares the same vision as Herder. Mazzini stresses, in a liberal manner, the equality of all individuals and races and their common human destiny. But this destiny should be realized through diversity. Mazzini takes the view that morality cannot be simply utilitarian nor be based on a narrow egoism. We have to work for and with others. Association is the key to human morality and progress. For it is only by cooperating with other individuals, within our families, nations and continents we will achieve a harmonious and fulfilled life. Mazzini ties his nationalist ethic to Christian beliefs. In trying to realize a world where cultural and ethnic ties are respected, we are no more than pressing for a world which God ordained.

Mazzini presents his liberal nationalist beliefs in a fascinating way in his *The Duties of Man*. Mazzini acknowledges in an enlightened manner that man's first duty 'is to humanity'.[16] But from this quasi-Kantian premiss Mazzini ingeniously reduces our first duty to a particular manifestation of humanity. As Mazzini sees it, humanity is too vast for us to consider it the object of our loyalty. We need something more manageable. The nation provides the essential mediating point between the individual and humanity. God has 'divided humanity into distinct groups on the face of the globe, and thus planted the seeds of nations'.[17]

Given God's inheritance to the human race Mazzini had then to explain how the world came to be divided up in such an unsatisfactory way in his own time. The existing non-national division of the globe was for Mazzini evidence of the ill will of our past rulers. 'Bad governments have disfigured the design of God which you may see so clearly marked out ... by the courses of the great rivers, by the lines of the lofty mountains, and by other geographical conditions.'[18] This neglect of God's true aspirations has for Mazzini to be made good. Mazzini was all for redrawing the map of Europe.

Like Herder, Mazzini stresses that human individuality expresses itself best in community with others. 'Without country,' he says, 'you have neither name, token, voice, nor rights, no admission as brothers into the fellowship of peoples.' He says of his own Italian people: 'You are the bastards of humanity.'[19] For Mazzini national liberation is not simply one further step in the emancipation of human individuals it is the necessary first step.

In Mazzini's view the nationalist cause takes precedence over all other political causes. Mazzini was aware of the growing appeal of socialism to the Italian masses, their desire for material distributive justice. His belief was, however, that material improvement could not be made without first addressing the national question. The inability of Italians to enjoy full national rights would forever condemn them to a second-class status. To enjoy fully the fruits of modern society the people to which you belong must itself belong to the international community. The common good cannot be realized through the political activity of a class, it can only be realized through the country to which one belongs.[20]

Mazzini shares the same view as Herder that nationality and territory go together. This conviction leads Mazzini to a powerful irredentism. 'Your country is one and indivisible. As the members of a family cannot rejoice at the common table ... so you should have no joy or repose as long as a portion of the territory upon which your language is spoken is separated from the Nation.'[21] National unity is both an ideal at which to aim and a reality that can be attained. 'A country is a fellowship of free and equal men bound together in a brotherly concord of labour towards a single end.'[22] For Mazzini a country should not be seen in a utilitarian way, simply as a stable social network within which to pursue our private aims. 'A country,' he says, 'is not an aggregation, it is an association.'[23]

Mazzini is a devout Christian and is drawn therefore to religious images. As Mazzini sees it, 'your country should be your temple. God at the summit, a people of equals at the base'. But Mazzini draws back from any fanaticism that this might imply. His goal for the Italian people is the secular ideal of a representative democracy. Liberalism and nationalism are regarded as being in harmony with one another. In a manner reminiscent of Kant, Mazzini argues that 'the whole nation therefore should be, directly or indirectly, the legislator'.[24] Liberal institutions further and deepen the commitment of an individual to his country. Mazzini consequently favours the extension of the franchise, a countrywide educational system and the intervention of the state in the economy. A popular national sentiment can best be spread through universal education. The state should not be seen simply as a means of providing security but also as a community. The emotional commitment to this modernizing nation-state has its roots, as with Herder, in the family.

Mazzini sees the family as 'the cradle of humanity'. 'What the country is to humanity, the family must be to the country.'[25]

For both Herder and Mazzini justice has to be realized through the national community. Legal justice and distributive justice are important for Mazzini, but they can only be firmly founded when the political unit is the correct one. Legal justice and a fair distribution of resources require, in Mazzini's view, a state that is also a nation. In this respect the liberal nationalist Mazzini is very close to the position now favoured by many individuals and leaders in the territories formerly dominated by the Soviet Union. Nationalism, as portrayed by Herder and Mazzini, possesses a powerful emotional appeal but it is uncertain that the political realization of its aims brings about the benefits in terms of justice that are often asserted. The claims of nationalism pose a very difficult problem for political theory.

POLITICAL THEORY, PATRIOTISM AND JUSTICE

The relation between political experience and our reflection upon it is a complex one. Political ideologies are needed to mediate between political theory and political practice. Political theories need to be expressed in a way that can make them accessible to others.[26] We cannot go directly on from political philosophy to order the kind of society we want. Political and moral philosophy may tell us a great deal about the kind of society which is just and fair. However, the kind of factors that bring such a society into existence are empirical and contingent. We have to work with human society as we find it before us and its cultural, legal organization takes on an immense variety of forms. That right takes priority over the good means that we have to accept and work with states which function (however imperfectly) with the rule of law. Political theorists have to have regard for political history. Our experience tells us that where the rule of law has most often functioned is within the modern national state. People who live under the protection of the rule of law tend to find themselves in such national states and those who are without its protection most often live in other kinds of possibly feudal, theological or ideological states. Those outside the national legal state system have quite naturally envied the relative freedom of those within national states and have wanted to adopt it for themselves. Quite often also, as with Mazzini, they have envied the sense of identity and belonging that those living within nations which have their own states have enjoyed.

I think there are clear reasons for this desire to belong to a nation-state. Any social organization requires an element of potential self-sacrifice from amongst its members to make it a success. It may be that this possibility of sacrifice casts doubts upon the value of social organization, but the cynic should reflect that the potential for loss arises within the social situation itself and does not prevail outside that arrangement where there can be no winners and losers. In a non-social situation there are, in one sense, nothing but losers. The possibility of loss (or the sacrifice) I am talking about arises from the coherence of social organization. All may gain from social cooperation but some may gain more than others at all sorts of times and occasions. Members of a social organization have to accept and bear this possibility of loss if a society is to function and persist.

Social organization greatly increases our potential for achieving things. Pyramids, skyscrapers, bridges and telecommunications satellites would not get off the ground if everyone went their own way. Skyscrapers, bridges and telecommunications satellites have added to my enjoyment of life and a pyramid is fun to look at even if the experience of being in one can be skipped. However, the difficulty is that these greater gains which arise from social cooperation are differentially enjoyed, and that for all sorts of reasons. Those with poor eyesight are not going to benefit a great deal from the aesthetic beauty of pyramids, just as those with a low income are less likely to get to Chicago to enjoy skyscrapers at their best (unless they happen to live there). Typically a society offers a variety of means of being a success and not all are going to be successful in many respects and some in very few. The effects of misfortune and luck cannot be wished away from any form of social arrangement.

So someone can always regard herself or himself as losing out as another gains. The chances of legitimate good fortune in a complex society are enormous. This is one of the reasons why large-scale social cooperation is attractive. But some kind of social cement is necessary to allow this gain (and loss) to go on. Moreover, as a society develops so also do the opportunities for illegitimate gain. Law enforcement can root out a great deal of crime, but not all. But apparently illegitimate gain in a complex society is not confined to illegal action. Some may gain undeservedly through the actions of their colleagues, fellow family members and fellow citizens. You cannot legislate against or punish those who gain from the efforts of other individuals simply through their co-membership of a society. All complex social organizations give rise to 'free riders' who effectively share the public social benefits without paying the full cost.[27] They are an inbuilt risk or a sacrifice of all political and social organization.

However, this free-riding or element of sacrifice has to be kept under control if a society is to persist. Although often unavoidable, it cannot become part of the official ideology of a society to encourage free riders if that society is to flourish. A society needs an ideology which allows both for gain and loss on the part of its members. A society particularly requires an ideology which soothes over the possible sacrifice cooperation entails. This is where patriotism has historically played an important role. And it is from this patriotism that nationalism derives the legitimacy it possesses. Patriotism has provided an ideal of social organization rooted in a people's past which has identified individuals with one another on a non-utilitarian basis. A strictly utilitarian appeal to social harmony runs up against the complaint that I am benefiting non-deserving others by cooperating with others. The more short-term this utilitarian perspective is the more unstable will be the ensuing cooperation. Patriotism, in contrast, bases social cooperation on a long-term vision of a homogeneous group of people in a given territory. It seems then that such a homogeneously regarded group of people has the best chance of realizing justice. Justice can try to draw on an already naturally existing basis for solidarity.

Patriotism is then an important element in the realization of right or justice in the world. Legal justice seems to flourish with its presence as a habit of mind within a society. People expect publicly recognized rules to be respected within their territory and they are happy to see the law enforced by an independent judiciary and officers of the law. Patriotism is not though an overly emotional allegiance to your country as evidenced in certain kinds of nationalism. As Hegel was aware, the patriotism which backs up justice or right is not necessarily the kind of patriotism which makes itself evident in times of war when individuals are prepared to sacrifice themselves for their country. 'Patriotism is often understood to mean only a readiness for exceptional sacrifices and actions. Essentially, however, it is the sentiment which, in the relationships of our daily life and under ordinary conditions, habitually recognizes that the community is one's substantive groundwork and end.'[28] Rather patriotism of the most valuable kind is evidenced in the readiness of citizens to recognize the worth of everyday institutions, practices and customs in preserving social cohesion. The term which Hobbes might give to this readiness to cohere might be *complaisance*.[29] We might generally see it as a readiness to oblige or reciprocate with fellow-citizens.

We have to accept that historically patriotism has generally grown up within nation-centred states. So the basis of patriotism has quite often been ethnic. This is not always the case of course. The United States is a notable example of a multi-ethnic state where patriotism holds sway. In Europe Switzerland is an example of a multilingual (if not entirely multi-ethnic) state. But patriotism nonetheless does benefit from a similarity of ethnic background. To say this, however, is not to suggest that the surest basis of right can be found in the single-ethnic state. The pursuit of ethnicity for its own sake can undermine right. Right or justice is a relationship amongst individuals abstractly conceived not a relationship with a natural or physical basis. Right requires that certain freedoms be respected by all individuals, regardless of their family status, sex, race or nationality. They do not arise from certain natural relationships, rather they help govern those relationships. To say that we belong to an ethnic community does not establish that we have any rights in relation to that community.

It is quite understandable that with the breakdown of communism the people of Eastern Europe are seeking new forms of political legitimacy and new means for the realization of justice. The lack of effective legal justice under communism implies that priority has to be given to political structures which allow it to flourish. Here national ties which pre-date the communist regimes appear to offer an attractive opportunity to realize a new and just state. And since the economic deprivations forced upon Eastern European countries, as a result both of the mismanagement of state socialism and the sudden opening to western markets and goods, have led to a situation of exigency and sacrifice, it is sensible that individuals should seek groupings within which they are prepared to bear these sacrifices. Thus, in the context of post-communism the nation-based (or ethnic) state has appeared an attractive proposition.

To establish and maintain legal justice something like patriotism or its equivalent is necessary. The independently acting members of the modern state have to have some common ideology (however minimal) to bind them together. Social solidarity may be threatened unless there are some means of justifying the type of inevitable sacrifice (and possibility of gain) which social cooperation brings with it. But the nation and its common ideology is from my viewpoint a support for the abstract legal idea of justice and not its realization. The value of patriotism is that it is a means to an end greater than itself. Raising patriotism into an end in itself, as is done with most, if not all, forms of nationalism prejudices, as I see it, the most valuable contribution that patriotism can make to our common life. We should put the community first the better to realize and protect individual right and not because the community (or the nation) is seen as superior to the individual.

JUSTICE BETWEEN STATES

Now, right or justice can be threatened both internally and externally. It is threatened internally when individuals attempt to break, avoid or evade the law and possibly, more profoundly, when others are seen as successfully getting away with any of these three things. Patriotism, with or without an ethnic basis, can help counteract this threat. It can provide support for a proper system of legal punishment. But justice or right is also threatened externally by lawlessness in the international community. Where the rule of law is palpably not respected in the international community this creates a sense of insecurity which rubs off even on the most settled of national or multinational states. As Hobbes observed, international relations resemble the state of nature where there is no respect shown to the law of nations.[30] The answer to this is not necessarily to create an international state which will hold states in awe, in the manner in which the mighty *Leviathan* – the state – would hold men in awe in civil society. A more satisfactory answer, following Kant, is to see right within the state as being continuous with right amongst states.[31] Justice within states is connected with and dependent upon justice among states.

One feature of a just state is that it is founded upon the acceptance of the rule of law. But it is difficult to support the rule of law internally without also wishing to see it established externally. Proper internal procedures for recognizing law have to be matched up by a desire to see such procedures adopted externally. A tense international environment threatens open discussion domestically and the enlightened consideration of new laws and policies. Often in the name of security long-established and legally respected rights can be waived. Quite often the international situation provides ample justification for such abrogations of domestic justice. There is no immunity from the rupture of rights that may occur in other states and between other states. As Kant puts it in his essay on *Perpetual Peace*: 'the peoples of the earth have reached a stage of (narrower or broader) community where a violation of rights in one place is felt in all places'.[32]

Kant's answer to this dilemma, and it is an answer I want to recommend here, is that the notion of justice or right should be extended to *cosmopolitan* right. In other words, Kant argues that rationally considered all right is universal. Right or justice cannot be restricted by race, nationality or physical location. Rights pertain to the human individual as a member of the species and the organization of states and their organization in relation to each other have to be conceived as mechanisms for attaining this right. Kant argues that both domestic societies and world society have to be gradually reformed to the point where cosmopolitan right is realized. 'The idea of a right of world-citizenship (cosmopolitan right) is not a fantastic or overstrained version of right but a necessary amendment to the unwritten code of civil and international right, to the rights of man in general and thus to perpetual peace.'[33]

A notable feature of the recent revolutions in Eastern Europe was their commitment to peace. They broke out in the context of the ending of 40-year-old head-on collision between the world's two major powers called the Cold War. And, to my mind, the great and undisputed achievement of these revolutions was to put behind the human race global nuclear conflict. We cannot be sure how long this will last. But it can only last properly if a

global system of international right and justice comes into being which
carries with it the respect of states and their citizens. If Kant is correct, the
most valuable side-effect of this realization of international justice will be
that it will create the conditions for successful domestic justice. Those who
are concerned about justice would do well not to overlook the continuity
between the two. Marxism may have reached its denouement in the collapse
of communism in the Soviet Union and Eastern Europe but, it seems to me,
the one thing it did get right was its internationalism. Justice cannot parochially
be constructed within the one state. Where justice does not extend beyond
the boundaries of nations or states justice itself is prejudiced.

NOTES

1. An exception to this general picture is R. P. Wolff's interesting *In Defence of
    Anarchism*, Harper, New York, 1976
2. Cf. L. Kolakowski, *Main Currents of Marxism*, Vol. 2, Oxford University Press,
    Oxford, 1978, p.476: 'There can be no doubt that Lenin's insurrectionary
    policy and all his calculations were based on a firm expectation that the
    Russian Revolution would touch off a world revolution or at least a European
    one. This view was in fact share by all the Bolsheviks: there was no question
    of "socialism in one country" for the first few years after the Revolution.'
3. V. I. Lenin, *Imperialism, the Highest Stage of Capitalism*, Progress Publishers,
    Moscow, 1968, p.11
4. Ibid., p.12
5. Plato, *The Republic*, Penguin, Harmondsworth, 1969, p.182
6. A. Buchanan, *Marxism and Justice*, Rowman & Littlefield, New Jersey, 1982,
    pp.50–1
7. J. Locke, *Two Treatises of Government*, Dent, London, 1977, pp.140–1
8. J. G. Herder (ed. F. M. Barnard), *Herder on Social and Political Culture*,
    Cambridge University Press, Cambridge, 1969, p.317
9. Ibid., p.163
10. Ibid., p.161
11. Ibid., p.163
12. Ibid.
13. Ibid., p.164
14. Ibid., p.165
15. Ibid., p.324
16. G. Mazzini, *The Duties of Man*, Dent, London, 1961, pp.41 and 51
17. Ibid., p.52
18. Ibid.
19. Ibid., p.53
20. Ibid., p.55
21. Ibid.

22. Ibid., p.56
23. Ibid., p.57
24. Ibid.
25. Ibid., p.61
26. H. Williams, *Concepts of Ideology*, Harvester, Brighton, 1988, p.128: 'The student of ideology cannot stand empty-handed in the face of the visions of the good life incorporated in the ideologies under consideration. Taking advantage of the theories of ideology already to hand, each must build up a view of social thought which is beneficial to him or herself and the community.'
27. Cf. P. Dunleavy, *Democracy, Bureaucracy and Public Choice*, Harvester, London, 1991, pp.46–51
28. G. W. F. Hegel, *Philosophy of Right*, tr. T. M. Knox, Oxford, 1969, para. 268, p.164
29. T. Hobbes, *Leviathan*, Fontana, London, 1969, p.162
30. Ibid., p.309
31. I. Kant, *Metaphysics of Morals*, tr. M. Gregor, Cambridge University Press, 1992, p.123; *Akademische Ausgabe*, Vol. VI, p.311
32. I. Kant, *Political Writings*, tr. H. Nisbet, Cambridge University Press, 1977, pp.107–108, *Akademische Ausgabe*, Vol. VIII, p.360
33. I. Kant, *Political Writings*, p.108; *Akademische Ausgabe*, Vol. VIII, p.360

10 International Relations and the Reconstruction of Political Theory

There is a dialectical adage which goes that at some point purely quantitative changes lead to a qualitative change. This dialectical rule of thumb, puzzled about by thinkers as diverse as Hegel, Engels and Lenin, might not always apply but, in my view, something has happened to politics in the twentieth century which has produced a qualitative change from what in the first instance appeared only to be a quantitative change. Bit by bit the element of international politics involved in domestic politics has crept up, to the point where the majority of politics is now international politics. The boundary lines between domestic politics and world politics have moved, I suggest, from being blurred to now being indistinguishable.

I should not like to say when precisely I think this qualitative change took place but since this is, in the nature of the case, a speculative argument I should hazard a guess that the alteration took place at the end of the Second World War. Doubtlessly those who participated in the setting up of such organizations as the United Nations, the International Monetary Fund, the World Bank and the European Steel and Coal Community in the immediate post-war period did not have in mind such a qualitative transformation but it is possible now to suggest that a partial result of their labours has been the gradual extinction of a purely domestic politics. The United Nations provided a forum for the discussion of the issues of world politics and an attempt to regulate them; the International Monetary Fund provided the rudiments of a world monetary order; and the European Steel and Coal Community gave a successful start to the gradual process of Western European integration.

Of course this internationalization has not taken place solely at the political level. Indeed we might suggest that what is now taking place on the political stage merely marks an underlying change that has been occurring in human society for a far longer time. Many political thinkers (of whom Kant and Marx are fine examples) have earlier pointed out that some of the bases of human society were transforming in a transnational direction. Both Kant and Marx looked forward to a time where demographic, technological and economic changes would gradually create one global system. Kant, as we saw earlier, pointed to migration and the settlement of the remoter parts of the globe as the key to a qualitative change;[1] Marx in turn looked to the development of a world market for commodities as the catalyst for one world order.[2] Early functionalist theory in international relations, of which David Mitrany's is an example, continued a theme of anarchist thinking when it stressed how the growth of material and economic cooperation might lead to a more peaceful world order.[3]

For myself, I am with thinkers such as David Held and J. Rosenau who believe unequivocally that we have entered a new international stage in the development of politics and society. The advances of the twentieth century in the means of communication, the development of global commodity and financial markets, global fashions, the emergence of the transnational corporation and the worldwide bank have made it well nigh impossible for a purely domestic politics to flourish. One might indeed be tempted to advance the hypothesis that the more advanced a nation, the more international is its orientation. An autarkic path of national development seems now ruled out, even for the largest of states. Just as individuals are unavoidably social beings so now states are almost necessarily both national and international entities.

David Held's view is that we have to develop a new type of social and political theory to deal with this qualitative transformation. As he puts it, the previously dominant theory of the sovereign democratic state presupposes the 'idea of a "national community of fate" – a community which rightly governs itself and determines its own future. This idea is challenged fundamentally by the nature of the pattern of global interconnections and the issues that have to be confronted by a modern state. National communities by no means exclusively "programme" the actions, decisions and policies of their governments and the latter by no means simply determine what is right or appropriate for their own citizens alone.'[4] Held and Anthony Giddens have been in the forefront of trying to conceptualize society globally. And I share their belief that this is the direction in which political theory might usefully go.

For Anthony Giddens 'modernity is inherently globalizing'.[5] Giddens takes capitalist institutions as typical of modernity and these are institutions which have uprooted individuals from the countryside and brought them into large urban centres where production and distribution take place on a very large scale. Globalization Giddens describes as 'the intensification of worldwide social relations which link distant localities in such a way that local happenings are shaped by events occurring many miles away and vice versa'.[6] Industrialization first gave the impulse for this globalization process, but nowadays it is service industries, international finance and, above all, the communications revolution which give the process its impetus. One of the consequences of globalization, according to Giddens, is the rise of local nationalisms. As he puts it, 'the development of globalized social relations probably serves to diminish some aspects of nationalist feeling linked to nation-states (or some states) but may be causally involved with the intensifying of more localized nationalist sentiments'.[7] Following Giddens's argument it might be argued in the British context that whereas the rise of international social, economic and political interrelations may have lessened the appeal of British nationalism, it may paradoxically have enhanced the appeal of Scottish and Welsh nationalism. Giddens sees global society as exhibiting both totalizing and localizing tendencies. He also tends to connect the process with the Second World War and its aftermath. As Giddens trenchantly observes, 'two world wars attest to the way in which local conflicts become matters of global involvement'.[8]

I have taught political theory at a British (Welsh!) university for fifteen years or so and I have over that time found its focus largely to be domestic. In accepting this focus I have had the vague intimation that its insights were applicable both to internal and international politics. But there is not a great deal in political theory as it presently stands to back up this hunch. The classical texts in political theory and the majority of commentaries on those texts tend to concentrate heavily upon the construction and maintenance of internal order. The main focus of political theory tends to be the theory of the state and not interstate theory. The state-centred political theory of Hobbes, rather than the internationally-centred political theory of Kant provides the main model. Iain Hampsher-Monk's stimulating book *A History of Modern Political Thought* nicely demonstrates the predominant view of the subject. The text concentrates upon nine major thinkers in the history of political ideas: Hobbes; Locke; Hume; Rousseau; Burke; Bentham; Mill; Hegel and Marx, devoting a chapter also to the American *Federalist* writers. Although the book covers a wide range of topics, from Hobbes's popular psychology and theory of morality to Marx's economic theory of the collapse of capitalism, there is no systematic treatment of international issues nor is there any extended discussion of the problem of war. Interestingly, neither 'international' nor 'war' occurs in the book's index. This is not to imply any deficiency on the part of the author. Iain Hampsher-Monk accurately reflects the preoccupations of those who teach modern political theory. As a textbook in the subject the book has justifiably proved a success. The topics which are thoroughly aired represent the standard concerns of political theorists, e.g., property, human nature, sovereign authority, the social contract and liberty.

Hampsher-Monk's approach to political theory is heavily historical and focuses on particular thinkers.[9] Given that he adopts this generally accepted approach it might be argued that it is not surprising that a global view of politics fails to emerge. The method itself is personal and particular, rather than being international and general. World politics perhaps suffers a less harsh fate in another popular approach to political theory. This is the approach to political theory through the study of ideology.

Texts in modern political ideologies survey the main competing ideologies of modern times with doctrines such as socialism, liberalism and conservatism playing a central role. On the whole, the study of these powerful ideologies does not lead the authors to an international perspective. This in itself is interesting since there are highly significant international strands to both liberal and socialist thinking. However, the emergence of environmentalism or ecological thinking as a powerful ideology in recent decades does lead the subject in a more international direction. Most recent textbooks on political ideology now include a chapter on environmentalism or ecologism. Examples are Andrew Vincent's *Modern Political Ideologies* and Terence Ball and Richard Dagger's *Political Ideologies and the Democratic Ideal* where the international dimensions of green thinking are carefully noted. As Vincent remarks, 'the ecology perspective ... tends to combine, uniquely, both respect for local autonomy in communities and a global message'.[10] For many ecologists their standpoint implies a vision of politics which takes it beyond conventional boundaries. 'Bioregions are not national, ethnic, administrative or overtly political units, but rather ecologically and biologically sustainable units.'[11] The central role of the nation-state in political life is put under scrutiny by the ecological approach. This questioning is duly recorded by political theorists who focus their enquiries upon political ideologies, but as yet it has not altered the predominantly (generally, one) state-centred approach of these theorists.

There are many reasons why this might be so. Possibly the most striking historical reason for the present main focus of political theory is that one of the main achievements of political activity up to now is the modern sovereign state. Political theory has in its preoccupations mirrored this success. The following are some of the main items to be found in works upon political theory: the issue of political obligation (in other words why should one accept the authority of the state); the issue of the safeguarding of individual freedom and property; the question of political representation; the issue of social justice; and, finally, the question of individual rights. No doubt this sketchy list can be supplemented (I personally like to look closely at the problem of ideology as well). But there could be little controversy about the main thrust of the subject. At the core of political theory, as classically understood, has been the problem of the relationship between the individual and the state. Some thinkers have seen this relationship as mediated by corporations or social classes and others (mainly liberals) have seen it as an almost one-to-one relationship between the individual and social authority. Political theory has tackled the question of security and order primarily at this individual level and has generally, and quite rightly, come up with an account of citizenship to answer the difficulties raised.

To say that the main focus of political theory has been on the relationship between the individual and the state is not to say that other interesting issues have been ignored. Many political theorists have looked at the relationship between collective entities (e.g. interest groups) and the state and most past political theorists of note have devoted part of their work to a discussion of international issues. In the book *International Relations in Political Theory* I have paid some attention to the latter literature. Augustine and Aquinas devote attention to the issues of war and international relations as part of their universalist Christian interest in the fate of humankind. In early modern times Machiavelli presents the bare bones of the highly influential realist theory of international politics. His rules for the wise conduct of the *Prince* have been taken up by many writers on the topic. Later Hobbes added a further dimension to the realist view. And there are a host of modern political theorists from Rousseau to Marx who have given attention to the principal problems of international relations.

In its classical sense I have found political theory a good subject to teach. Its focus upon the state and citizenship is distinctive. The paths to follow are clearly marked out. There is a well-established tradition, so the syllabus almost chooses itself. Also the issues about which political theory speculates are concrete and live. The state functions in everyday life and individuals have in varying ways come to terms with it. In advocating forms of citizenship political theorists seem not to have been whistling in the dark. Societies through the ages have needed their message, or at least it might be said that societies have needed the choice of messages they have offered. Political theory, especially as it has flowed into political ideologies, has found a ready and continually expanding market.

It is difficult to see the requirement for this type of political theory entirely disappearing even with the internationalization of human society. Individuals will always have to relate to their more immediate societies and the best of political theories put forward some well-tried paths for individuals to follow. Citizenship has always to be a concern for political theory. But political theory has, I think, to change with the times. This is not simply a question of blindly following fashions. Just as political philosophy had once to accommodate itself to the development of the modern state and the problems of identity to which it gave rise, so now the subject has to take into account the globalization of human life. This is not a straightforward task because it is the essence of genuine novelty that in the first instance – before it is properly experienced – it leaves us with little to say.

The suggestion that political theory may need to undergo a radical change seems to contradict the most recent flowering of political theory which has taken place in the United States and Britain. After its apparent demise in the 1950s political theory has made a remarkable leap to prominence through the work of individuals like John Rawls, Robert Nozick, Bruce Ackerman, Brian Barry, Charles Taylor and, more polemically, Roger Scruton and the revival of Hayekian political thought which has occurred with the work of commentators like John Gray and Norman Barry. The focus of this recent writing has remained as ever upon the relationship between the individual and the state.[12] Rawls has given the idea of the social contract a new lease of life through interpreting it in a Kantian mode, Nozick has given greater credibility to libertarian neo-Conservatism by rethinking the idea of the state of nature, Ackerman has developed a plausible form of hardline liberalism and Taylor has given greater force to the contribution of classical political theorists as diverse as Augustine and Hegel.[13] Paradoxically, as Marx's practical influence withers over large tracts of the world his work remains a lively subject for debate in many European and North American universities.

All this adds up to a very stimulating and still relevant literature. The great advantage that this kind of political theory possesses – which concentrates on the relationship between the individual and state – is that you can go straight out and do it. Every individual can try out for herself or himself the views of citizenship advanced. Personal ethical deliberation or individual utilitarian calculation is often at the heart of these theories. With this kind of political theory you can reject or accept theories according to your personal experience. I have no wish to deny that this represents a remarkable flowering of the subject but I nonetheless feel this kind of political theory may have its limitations. Long-time students of international relations would probably agree with me here. Such students might likely see the deep concerns about individual autonomy, and social choice, evident in recent political theory as remote and almost irrelevant to the changes occurring in international society. The individualist, voluntarist assumptions of political theory would seem to be out of touch with the realities of international relations where choice seems, at best, to be severely limited.[14] This sense of distance which might occur to the specialist in international relations (perhaps particularly a specialist of the realist school) is to be regretted. The gap between international relations and political theory needs to be bridged. Advanced political theory needs, I think, to grapple with the exigencies of international relations just as much as students of international relations need to take advantage of the intellectual rigour and robustness of political theory.

It is, however, already to overstate the problem when it is suggested that international relations and political theory have to be drawn together. They are not on closer inspection such remote intellectual preoccupations. I have tried to show in my *International Relations in Political Theory* how classical political theory, taken from a new perspective, has a great deal to say about the problems of international relations. And it is possibly only the novice in the study of international relations who might suggest that international relations thinkers have been unaware of the value and insights of political theory. Hans Morgenthau, one of the most influential writers in international relations, also taught political theory. It is difficult also not to be impressed by the grasp of political theory shown by prominent international relations writers like Stanley Hoffmann and Kenneth Waltz. Waltz's highly influential *Man, the State and War* draws extensively from traditional political theory and Stanley Hoffman finds in Rousseau a valuable classical source for the contemporary study of international relations.[15] There is then already a confluence of the two 'streams' of thought.

I want here to suggest what this confluence implies for the study of political theory. It may be taken for granted that I do not wish to see the excellent tradition of political theory abandoned. The challenges of thinking a radically altering world require as their foundation the insights of earlier political thought. But political theory will not do as it stands. We cannot, I think, use a solely nation-state-centred theory to look at a world which is becoming rapidly less nation-state centred. One thing which makes John Rawls's seminal *A Theory of Justice* problematic for me is his assumption that the appropriate form of distributive justice should first be decided on a national basis.[16] This is a very valuable thought-exercise and it may be extended to a global context but it seems to me that the whole procedure might put the cart before the horse. From the standpoint of an interdependent world it might be better to begin with a theory of global distributive justice and then see what implications this might have at a national level.

It is interesting to note that John Rawls has recently himself turned his attention to the problem of world order. In his lecture 'The Law of Peoples' he attempts to sketch how a basic structure for international relations might be deduced from the the approach to domestic politics he outlines in *A Theory of Justice*. Rawls argues that an implication of his approach is that 'not all regimes can reasonably required to be liberal, otherwise the law of peoples itself would not express liberalism's own principle of toleration for other reasonable ways of ordering society'.[17] He believes that a parallel can be drawn between the relations which individuals might rationally be expected to accept amongst themselves and the relations that states might rationally be expected to adopt. In his view, 'just as a citizen in a liberal society must respect other persons' comprehensive religious, philosophical, and moral doctrines provided they are pursued in accordance with a reasonable political conception of justice, so a liberal society must respect other societies organized by comprehensive doctrines, provided their political and social institutions meet certain conditions that lead the society to adhere to a reasonable law of peoples'.[18] This is an imaginative procedure that Rawls adopts, but it is interesting to note that the procedure, like *A Theory of Justice*, moves out from the domestic conditions of justice to try to establish the international conditions of justice. Rawls assumes a hiatus between the domestic conditions of justice and the international conditions for justice. Political theory and international relations are here kept at a discrete distance from one another.

It seems appropriate at this point to say a word on behalf of Lenin. In the last few years we have seen the discrediting of Marxism-Leninism justifiably reaching its height in Europe and Russia. But before Lenin is consigned to the 'rubbish heap' of history I should like to do something to salvage his reputation as a political theorist. I should like to suggest that his essay on *Imperialism* represents one of the first serious attempts by a political theorist to think through the implication of the *internationalization* of human society. If many of the practical consequences of Lenin's thinking were disastrous, this does not mean that his theory was entirely misplaced. The question of the best relation between theory and practice in politics is a very tricky one, and Lenin was possibly not the first to get it wrong. But taken as a theory his view of the economic roots of imperialism is a plausible one. More impressive perhaps is the way he conceives of society globally and seeks out the possible links between political and military crises in one corner of the earth with financial and industrial difficulties in other corners of the world. Lenin's view of the interconnectedness of world politics and world economics and the interconnectedness of national and global politics fits in well with what is happening today.[19] From the perspective Lenin adopted it might not seem in the least surprising that a referendum in France would lead to the devaluation of the Italian lira and a run on the pound in Britain. Indeed, Lenin might well have produced the script for a drama very similar to the one which occurred with the European monetary crisis of 1992. The intertwining of national and international political events and the simultaneous nature of the economic and political crises of the time were very close to the type of global crises Lenin depicted occurring in *Imperialism*. Lenin's problem is that he perhaps made too much of this drama of international and national politics and sought in the proletariat a (collective) hero to bring the plot to a successful conclusion. But he has to be applauded for seeing possible links where others seemingly saw only turmoil and discontinuity.

Lenin's account of capitalist imperialism demonstrates one manner in which political theory and the study of international relations can be valuably brought together. Indeed the political theory and the theory of international relations cannot be distinguished in this tract of Lenin's. For Lenin the movements of finance capital condition the actions of states both from within and without. But for obvious reasons this is not the kind of general synthesis between the two approaches that everyone would accept. It appears that a precondition for seeing world society entirely along the lines that Lenin suggests is that you have to be a Marxist.

What appears to have happened from about the time of Lenin's essay (first published in 1917) is that political theory and international relations have gone their separate ways. Prominent political theorists have retained their focus on the state from its internal side, and thinkers about international relations have inclined to look at the state from its external side. A division of labour developed in which those interested in 'politics' looked at the mirror of the state from the one side and those interested in international relations looked at the mirror of the state from the other side. This led to a kind of mutual blindness in which political theorists regarded international relations as a novel field for gifted amateurs and international relations thinkers regarded political theory as one specialism amongst others from which they might draw in putting together their view of the world. For myself I think it may be more helpful to view the relationship between international relations and political theory *symbiotically*. Political theory might then be seen as a rich source for international relations theory and international theory might be seen as a new and exciting field for political theorists. I shall try briefly to sketch why I think this is so, first from the political theory side and then from the international relations side.

POLITICAL THEORY FOR INTERNATIONAL RELATIONS

Many writers on international politics think that Hobbes's account of the state of nature presents a useful analogy of the condition of states in international relations. Hobbes might then be regarded as providing an early justification of the realist view of international politics. The principles underlying Morgenthau's *Politics among Nations* appear to follow closely this analogy with Hobbes. Thus, Hobbes's expectations of the state of nature might be taken to fall in well with the policy conclusions which the realist draws. Morgenthau's first assumption that 'society is in general, governed by objective laws that have their roots in human nature' mirrors almost precisely Hobbes's model of political science.[20] And Morgenthau's second assumption which equates power with interest, or the pursuit of power with the pursuit of interest, relates very closely to the primacy given to self-preservation in Hobbes's political philosophy.[21] Also Morgenthau's strongly expressed view that politics forms an autonomous sphere seems to draw upon Hobbes's assumption that political sovereignty must take precedence over individual conceptions of justice. Hobbes undeniably sees the state of nature as a state of continuous friction and conflict. But there is more to Hobbes's political theory than this seemingly stark realism. As Beitz shows, Hobbes not only has certain prescriptions as to how the insecurities of the state of nature can be overcome but he has also other clear views about international relations which flow from his analysis of the state of nature.[22]

Part of the reason for the hiatus between political theory and international relations comes from the tradition of political theory itself. Hobbes's *Leviathan* can be read as a theory of individual survival under negative social conditions. Generally, commentaries by political theorists look at Hobbes's philosophy from the standpoint of rational action on the individual's part.[23] But the *Leviathan* might also be read as a theory of the survival of societies under difficult circumstances, leading to an account of the type of social structure, which is required to allow prosperity. Hobbes may himself have begun from and emphasized the individual perspective, but we can read him differently placing more emphasis on the social and state perspective.

Hobbes himself gives a clue as to how this might be done. He suggests the precarious position in which the individual finds himself in the *Leviathan* can be read as one and the same for the society of which he is part.[24] Hobbes believes that the individual state of nature, which he describes so graphically at the beginning of the the *Leviathan* can be regarded as analagous with the condition of relations among states. Sovereign nations, with regard to one another, may be regarded as in an international state of nature. The stratagems he puts forward for order and success can, in his opinion, be applied equally by the leaders of states in their relations with one another. Now the mistake is easily made from the international relations perspective that the consequence of adopting Hobbes's model is that we have also to recommend an international state or a *Leviathan* to maintain world peace. But this is not entirely what the model implies. When the model is looked at closely other interesting implications flow from it which may be of some relevance to international relations.

Hobbes's own prescription for international society is in fact not one Leviathan to maintain order. Rather he suggests that from the anarchy of the relations among states an order might be gradually established which draws from the laws of nature. These laws of nature are ones which Hobbes sees as applying among individuals in the absence of state power. The observance of these laws is indeed voluntary but in observing them individuals will add both to their own security and the security of other individuals. In parallel with this states (or their leaders) may see themselves as bound by these natural laws. Hobbes puts forward a dozen or so laws of nature which might well provide a beginning in the gradual creation of a peaceful world order.

The basis for Hobbes's laws of nature is the rational pursuit of self-interest. He shows that self-interest need not be identical with selfishness. 'A law of nature, *lex naturalis*, is a precept or general rule, found out by reason, by which a man is forbidden to do that, which is destructive of his life, or taketh away the means of preserving the same; and to omit that, by which he thinketh it may best be preserved.' Whereas the second law of nature gives precedence to self-preservation in the face of an external threat, the first law of nature requires us to 'seek peace, and follow it'.[25] Hobbes expects neither individuals nor states simply to sacrifice their existence on the behalf of others. In seeking to maintain peace we are also allowed to defend ourselves by all means possible. But the third law of nature balances this apparent licence in that it advocates reciprocity in one's relationship with others.[26] Mutual restraint and aid can add considerably to the well-being of both parties. Many of Hobbes's other laws of nature demonstrate how this mutuality can be sustained and broadened. The fifth law of nature, for instance, calls for 'complaisance'.[27] By complaisance Hobbes means that individuals and states should seek to accommodate themselves to others. The advantage of being obliging towards other states is that we may expect such behaviour in return. This we can often achieve without putting ourselves in the least danger. As I have tried to show in my *International Relations in Political Theory*, with Hobbes's laws of nature we have practical rules of conduct which may considerably enhance relations among states.[28]

Whereas previously those who have taught political theory (possibly because they have been heavily influenced by the perspectives and problems of citizenship) have seen the chapter on the *state* of nature as the most likely central one in the *Leviathan*, I suggest that those who wish to teach a restructured political theory might see the chapter on the *laws* of nature as the more central one. In this chapter a different Hobbes emerges from the one that is apparent in the chapter on the condition of man. The international perspective fits in better with chapters 14 and 15 on the Laws of Nature. Here Hobbes does not appear as indifferent to world peace and harmony. The aim of survival is not pursued at the expense of sociability. Rather the two aims are simultaneously pursued.

Reinterpreting Hobbes in this way might be seen as being akin to the kind of reinterpretation that occurs to the works of great artists. Up to now Hobbes's identity in political theory seems to have been fixed in a manner which is unusual for a great artist and his work in the history of art. In the study of art Picasso's blue period might at one time be regarded as the most central stage in his development. At another time, however, Picasso's realist stage might be the most highly regarded. Other students of art might find the abstract period Picasso shared with Braque as the most engaging. There is no reason then why the more peaceable side of Hobbes's *Leviathan* might not be legitimately seen as the key to his political thought.

INTERNATIONAL RELATIONS FOR POLITICAL THEORY

An example we might take of the relevance of international relations for political theory is in the recent work of James Rosenau. In his book *Turbulence in World Politics* Rosenau points to the need for international relations to adopt different perspectives if it is to think through properly current changes. He thinks the boundaries between domestic and international politics are breaking down and as a consequence the billiard-ball model of relations among states should be set to one side. For Rosenau states are not like the various distinct pieces in a chess game with their own characteristics and capabilities, rather their capabilities and characteristics are interdependent. Thus for Rosenau there can be no pure theories of domestic politics just as there can be no pure theories of international relations. He regards us as now being in a period of post-international relations which calls for one integrated theory of the state and interstate relations. As he puts it, 'the very notion of "international relations" seems obsolete in the face of an apparent trend in which more and more of the interactions that sustain world politics unfold without the direct involvement of nations or states. So a new term is needed, one that denotes the presence of new structures and processes while at the same time allowing for still further structural developments. A suitable label would be postinternational politics.'[29]

This is a challenging thesis and one with which I find myself in almost complete agreement. A reservation I would make concerns only the apparent enormity of the task that Rosenau sets for himself. Developing an interpretation of politics that deals successfully both with national and international order is an extraordinarily ambitious proposition. I tend to think of it as a field to be worked upon by a large number of individuals rather than one that can be dealt with by the one theorist. But Rosenau does not avoid the issue and has himself a number of things to say about the nature of such a theory.

Rosenau sees the present post-international condition as beginning after the Second World War. Continuous change is one of the hallmarks of the present condition, leading to uncertainty and doubt about existing institutions and future relations. Rosenau's choice of the term turbulence to denote this condition is intended to convey that the process of change is not sudden nor without limit. Rosenau does not want to depict international relations as in a continuous process of revolution, rather he wants to suggest a regularity which is subject to periodic disturbance. Rosenau attributes this turbulence to a fundamental shift in international relations. The nature of this shift which is taking place and brings turbulence is one which undermines the previously dominant role of the sovereign state in world politics. For Rosenau 'the transformation is marked by a bifurcation in which the state-centric system now coexists with an equally powerful, though more decentralized, multi-centric system'.[30]

The conception of international relations which is being undermined by the move to post-international politics is sometimes described as that of the 'Westphalian order'.[31] By this is meant the order of European states which emerged after the Peace Treaty of Westphalia of 1648. Before that time Europe is regarded as being dominated by a medieval system in which there was some transnational control of political relations through institutions such as the Catholic Church and the Hapsburg monarchy. In this earlier period political power was held by the nobility, reflecting their dominance of the economic system through feudalism. The Westphalian system of post-1648 became global through the Europeanization of the world fuelled by the rapid development of capitalism. The capitalist economic system first took root in Europe, but was from its inception (as we have seen with Locke) in the city-states of Italy and the commercial trading centres of the European coastal states, an expanding transnational economic order.

Although global in its reach this Westphalian international system did not give rise to a global system of order. The political order which arose from the Westphalian system depended very much on the states themselves. In this system each state was regarded as independent of the other and its relations with others were conditioned as much by force as morality. The Westphalian system gave rise to a system of international law, but it was not a legal system which was always respected and upheld by the states subject to it. This is because the sovereign state lay at the heart of the Westphalian system and this implied that ultimately the leaders of states were free to give a higher priority to the pursuit of their policy objectives than to the observance of the rules of international law. As a consequence of this, under the Westphalian system, the rule of law operates in a partial and incomplete way. It operates amongst those states who wish to observe it and may also operate for those states who have the power to enforce it. Those states without the power to enforce the rules of international law have to depend upon the law-abiding nature of other states. This Westphalian order was a contradictory and confusing system and was possibly ripe for change.

If we are to believe Rosenau this Westphalian order has left a legacy of state-centredness which it is very difficult to remove. We have seen that political theory is still largely a state-centred mode of enquiry where the nature of one internal sovereign order is closely examined. But, according to Rosenau, 'students of world politics, like politicians, are prisoners of their parameters, unwilling or unable to escape the premise of state predominance and constantly tempted to cling to familiar assumptions about hierarchy, authority and sovereignty'.[32] Rosenau does not believe that this state-centredness should be combated simply by throwing out the idea, rather he thinks the idea of state-centredness should be combined with a multicentric approach. As Rosenau sees it, in current international relations state influences are diminishing but not marginal.[33] He advocates a two-world conception of global politics where state influence is seen in the context of interdependence and international regimes such as that brought about by the International Monetary Fund and the General Agreement on Tarriffs and Trade. Rosenau quotes the political scientist Karl Deutsch to suggest in the current circumstances of the world the 'state has become both indispensable and inadequate'.[34]

Essential to Rosenau's theory of post-international politics is the notion of 'powerful people'.[35] By powerful people Rosenau does not mean the traditional elites that have governed human society. Rather Rosenau believes that the worldwide changes in communication, technology and education have empowered every individual. The dependency of the world economy on the advance in knowledge and understanding means that everyone is potentially a valuable resource. Individuals have in their own capabilities a powerful lever of change. It is almost impossible to deny individuals the information that will lead to their advance, and with their new insights they will require their governments to change in the direction of the most appealing global standards. Rosenau sees two powerful but contrary tendencies asserting themselves at present in world society. On the one hand, there is a centralizing tendency brought about by global interdependence and, on the other hand, there is a decentralizing tendency brought about by a desire to establish a particular regional identity. Rosenau refers to this latter tendency as 'sub-groupism'.[36]

Like Anthony Giddens, Rosenau thinks world politics is subject to two powerful and counteracting forces. Giddens sees it as a tension between the local and the global. Rosenau sees it as a tension between the needs of the 'sub-group' or the requirements of the 'sub-system' and the needs and requirements of an interdependent world. For Rosenau 'environmental pollution, currency crises, terrorism, and the other new issues growing out of greater interdependence impel coordination among systems even as the information revolution, global television, the proliferation of service activities, continued elaboration of the division of labour, and the other features of the post-industrial era, decentralize the loci of action, enhance the influence of sub-systems, and enlarge the role of citizens'.[37]

One can well see that Rosenau might draw on contemporary theories of nationalism to fill out this concept. And once one intellectually breaks down the barriers between internal and international politics in the way in which Rosenau does there are very many aspects of traditional political theory, like the theory of nationalism, which present themselves as obvious sources for thinking about current international relations. To round off the chapter I should like to look at one such aspect.

FREEDOM AND INTERNATIONAL RELATIONS

Freedom or liberty is a continuing and justifiable concern of political theory. A distinction that political theorists often invoke is, as we saw in Chapter 5, the distinction between positive and negative freedom. Those who stress this distiction tend, almost counter-intuitively, to regard the negative view of freedom more favourably (or positively) and the positive view of freedom less favourably (or negatively). Negative freedom is presented as a freedom from and positive freedom is presented as a freedom to. Liberal political theorists, like Isaiah Berlin, see absence of restraint upon the individual's activities as at the heart of human freedom.[38] For Berlin freedom is not only liberty to do the right thing, it is also from time to time liberty to do the wrong thing. Berlin sees a positive view of freedom, which puts forward best modes of living one's life, as too overbearing and leading too readily to the interference of the state and others in one's life. The interesting thing about this discussion from the present point of view is that it focuses on the relation between the individual and the state. One of the main objects of those who advocate the negative view is, for example, to ward off the threat of totalitarianism. The theory was advanced under circumstances where the greatest pressure upon the freedom of action of the individual appeared to come from a once prevalent totalitarian conception of the domestic state. But nowadays it appears that international institutions put as much pressure on the liberty of individuals and in some instances are seen as offering the best opportunity for the improvement of liberty. There is a strongly held view apparent in British politics at present that the institutions of the European Community represent a challenge to the independence of individuals and corporations. Many politicians, rightly or wrongly, feel that the European Commission acts upon a positive view of freedom which runs counter to the traditions of British life. In contrast, some of the citizens of the former Yugoslav state tend to see in the institutions of the Economic Community their best future chance for prosperity and freedom. They may well enthusiastically embrace the positive conception of freedom detected by some in the ethos of the European Community.

In the light of developments such as these, it seems that debates about the virtues and vices of positive and negative freedom which focus solely upon domestic institutions may become somewhat abstract. Increasingly individuals pursue freedom in a regional or global context. Comparisons with worldwide standards of freedom and individual opportunity appeared to have played a large part in the collapse of communism. There may not yet be universal standards of freedom and justice but it nonetheless seems that individuals and societies increasingly aspire to such standards. This is not meant to imply that the earlier debates in political theory about freedom can simply be set to one side. In many respects those debates provided the framework within which events have unfolded in Europe and the rest of the world in the modern epoch. Rather what I think might be usefully done is for these debates to be refashioned in the wider context of globally interconnected human society. Questions about positive and negative liberty come into play in relations with organizations such as the United Nations and European Community as well as with the domestic state.

What I have said about freedom might well be thought to apply more strongly to the question of rights. Much of the debate of modern political theory has been constructed in terms of rights, originally taken to be natural rights. Historically, individuals have (quite sensibly) demanded rights in relation to their own nation-states. They may have based these demands upon a universal view of human nature, as did the American and French revolutionaries, but these advocates of rights were seemingly in no doubt that it was their own state which should guarantee and safeguard these rights. But the picture nowadays seems to have changed. Rights are not solely asserted in relation to the domestic state. Rights are often asserted by individuals as part of the international community. Natural rights have been transformed into human rights, supposedly universally valid. As Leslie Macfarlane expresses it, 'human rights are those moral rights which are owed to each man or woman by every man or woman solely by reason of being human'.[39] There is a most impressive literature in international political theory on the issue of rights. This issue was given great impetus as a global concern by the Universal Declaration of Human Rights of 1948. Side by side with the development of a global ideology of human rights there have developed global pressure groups like Amnesty International to press the cause. As the political theorist Norman Barry puts it: 'Rights are now not merely asserted defensively against state action but are interpreted as legitimate claims upon government to satisfy human needs.'[40]

The topic of rights represents common ground for political theory and international relations. This remarkable coincidence of interests can be seen in the following comments from specialists in the two respective fields. According to the political theorist Michael Freeden, 'the concept of rights has become one of the most reputable and positively connoted in political theory. The desirability of promoting in principle the ideas represented by the concept is far less controversial than, for example, the promotion of equality, democracy or even liberty. Only a minority of viewpoints, such as the Marxist critique and extreme versions of consequentialism, point to the possibility that adherence to rights might cause social or human damage. Modern Political theory, which may be said to have begun with Hobbes, locates the notion of rights at the centre of its debates.'[41] To be compared with Freeden's views are those of R. J. Vincent, a theorist of international relations. According to Vincent, 'there are a number of senses in which it might be said that the theory of world politics – theory here as a reflection on the public arrangements that ought to be made for the government of mankind – should start with human rights'.[42] Both theorists therefore argue for the centrality of rights in their disciplines.

The reasons for this centrality in international relations are, for Vincent, twofold. First, 'human rights are the rights that everybody should have by virtue of his or her very humanity. Any political theory [sic!] that disregarded them, therefore, would make the mistake of overlooking a political axiom.'[43] Secondly, 'since the seventeenth century, human rights or natural rights have been a conventional liberal starting-place for political theory, so that in pursuing reason we would be following tradition'.[44] Here the boundary lines between the two disciplines are not so much overlooked by Vincent as consciously removed. The universality of rights claims makes it almost impossible to confine our enquiries to the sphere of the one sovereign state. New rights gained in one state indirectly produce demands for the same rights in other states. Citizens of those states with the highest standards of right are envied by the citizens and subjects of less fortunate states. International comparisons are inevitable and world standards (whether or not they are fully met) inevitably emerge.

The title of this chapter, 'international relations and the reconstruction of political theory' may have suggested that I was intending to set out an agenda for political theory and international relations. This is not so. I don't think changes in the approaches of disciplines come about simply by such advocacy. What I am trying to do is a lot less dramatic. I think I am setting out an agenda that is already with us. This is the agenda I seek to convey with the title of the book, which speaks of international relations and the limits of political theory. It seems to me that international relations theorists and political theorists are already beginning to think along the lines I suggest. I see myself as articulating a trend, rather than bringing one into being.

NOTES

1. I. Kant, *Perpetual Peace* in L. W. Beck, (ed. and translator), *Kant Selections*, p.441; *Akademische Ausgabe* VIII, p.363
2. 'The need of a constantly expanding market for its products chases the bourgeoisie over the whole surface of the globe. It must nestle everywhere, settle everywhere, establish connexions everywhere. The bourgeoisie has through its exploitation of the world market given a cosmopolitan character to production and consumption in every country.' K. Marx, and F. Engels, *Communist Manifesto*, Progress Publishers, Moscow, 1969, p.46
3. Cf. P. R. Viotti and M. V. Kauppi, *International Relations Theory*, Macmillan, New York, 1990, pp.206–7
4. D. Held, *Political Theory Today*, Polity Press, Oxford, 1991, p.202
5. A. Giddens, *The Consequences of Modernity*, Polity Press, Oxford, 1990, p.63
6. Ibid., p.64
7. Ibid., p.65
8. Ibid., p.77
9. I. Hampsher-Monk, *A History of Modern Political Thought*, Blackwell, Oxford, 1992: 'Whilst not entirely suppressing the authorial voice I have tried to reflect the different preoccupations of current research on the various authors.' p.x
10. A. Vincent, *Modern Political Ideologies*, Blackwell, Oxford, 1992, p.225. Cf. T. Ball and R. Dagger, *Political Ideologies and the Democratic Ideal*, HarperCollins, New York, 1995, p.234
11. A. Vincent, *Modern Political Ideologies*, p.230
12. For a good recent survey see R. Plant, *Modern Political Theory*, Blackwell, Oxford, 1991
13. J. Rawls, *A Theory of Justice*, Oxford University Press, Oxford, 1972; R. Nozick, *Anarchy, State and Utopia*, Blackwell, Oxford, 1974; B. Ackerman, *Social Justice in the Liberal State*, Yale University Press, New Haven, 1980; C. Taylor, *Sources of the Self*, Cambridge University Press, Cambridge, 1979
14. This view is expressed by M. Wight in his article 'Why is there no International Theory' in H. Butterfield and M. Wight, (eds) *Diplomatic Investigations*, Allen & Unwin, London, pp.17–34
15. K. Waltz, *Man, the State and War*, Columbia University Press, New York, 1959; S. Hoffman and D. Fidler (eds), *Rousseau on International Relations*, Oxford University Press, 1991
16. J. Rawls, *A Theory of Justice*, p.8. Cf. T.W. Pogge, *Realizing Rawls*, Cornell University Press, New York, 1989, p.240

17. J. Rawls, 'The Law of Peoples', in S. Shute and S. Hurley, *On Human Rights*, Basic Books, New York and London, 1994, p.43

18. J. Rawls, 'The Law of Peoples', p.43

19. Cf. V. I. Lenin, *Imperialism*, Progress Publishers, Moscow, 1971, p.9: 'Capitalism has grown into a world system of colonial oppression and of the financial strangulation of the overwhelming majority of the population of the world by a handful of "advanced" countries.' The point is put rather luridly but not without a degree a validity.

20. H. Morgenthau, *Politics among Nations*, Knopf, New York, 1973, p.5

21. Ibid.

22. C. Beitz, *Political Theory and International Relations*, Princeton University Press, 1979, pp.50–1

23. Cf. D. P. Gauthier, *The Logic of the Leviathan*, Oxford University Press, 1979; J. Hampton, *Hobbes and the Social Contract Tradition*, Cambridge University Press, Cambridge, 1990

24. T. Hobbes, *Leviathan*, Fontana, London, 1969, pp.309–10: 'Concerning the offices of one sovereign to another, which are comprehended in that law, which is commonly called the law of nations, I need not say anything in this place; because the law of nations, and the law of nature, is the same thing. And every sovereign hath the same right , in procuring the safety of his people, that any particular man can have, in procuring the safety of his own body.'

25. Ibid., p.146

26. Ibid., p.147: 'that a man be willing, when others are so too, as far-forth, as for peace, and defence of himself he shall think it necessary, to lay down this right to all things; and be contented with so much liberty agains other men, as he would allow other men against himself.'

27. Ibid., p.162: 'A fifth law of nature, is complaisance; that is to say, that every man strive to accommodate himself to the rest. For the understanding whereof, we may consider, that there is in men's aptness to society, a diversity of nature, rising from their diversity of affections; not unlike to that we seen in stones brought together for building an edifice. For as that stone which by the asperity, and irregularity of figure, takes more room from others, than itself fills; and for the hardness, cannot be easily made plain, and thereby hindreth the building, is by the builders cast away as unprofitable, and troublesome: so also, a man by asperity of nature, will strive to retain those things which to himself are superfluous, and to others necessary; and for the stubbornness of his passions, cannot be corrected, is to be left, or cast out of society, as cumbersome thereto.'

28. H. L. Williams, *International Relations in Political Theory*, Open University Press, Buckingham, 1991, pp.64–5

29. J. Rosenau, *Turbulence in World Politics*, Princeton University Press, New Jersey, 1990, p.6

30. Ibid., p.11

31. D. Held, 'Democracy: from City-State to a Cosmopolitan Order', in D. Held, (ed.) *Prospects for Democracy*, Blackwell, Oxford, 1992, p.24

32. J. Rosenau, *Turbulence in World Politics*, p.244

33. Ibid., p.247

34. Ibid., p.249

35. Ibid., ch.13

36. Ibid., p.132
37. Ibid., p.253. A very similar thesis is advanced by J. Camilleri, and J. Falk, in *The End of Sovereignty*, Edward Elgar, Aldershot, 1992
38. I. Berlin, *Four Essays on Liberty*, Oxford University Press, 1969, p.171
39. L. Macfarlane, *The Theory and Practice of Human Rights*, Maurice Temple Smith, London, 1985, p.3
40. N. Barry, *An Introduction to Modern Political Theory*, Macmillan, London, 1989, p.226
41. M. Freeden, *Rights*, Open University Press, Buckingham, 1991, p.1
42. R. J. Vincent, *Human Rights and International Relations*, Cambridge University Press, Cambridge, 1986, p.111
43. Ibid.
44. Ibid.

11 Conclusion

In suggesting there are limits to political theory as conventionally understood I do not wish to claim this in a dismissive or strongly negative sense. For I also think that there are considerable strengths to political theory as traditionally practised and I am ready to acknowledge that those virtues may only have arisen as a consequence of the self-imposed limits that those who work in that tradition respect. Political theory is a scholarly enterprise which concentrates upon the discussion of problems of public order and cooperation taken both from a contemporary and historical point of view. The history of political thought is important to the political theorist. Those dealing with current issues try to embed their discussions in past debate.

My argument is not that this tradition is wrong but rather that now might be an appropriate time to reconsider those limits. A traditional focus of political theory is the domestic or national state. My view is that this national state is changing so rapidly under the pressure of international markets, international communications and international culture that it it is difficult to sustain a political theory which is wholly internal in its emphasis.

I should like to turn briefly to Habermas's recent political theory to illustrate my point. Habermas's theory of the democratic state begins from the domestic perspective but leads in a wider international direction. This happens because he follows through the logic of his own discourse ethics and participatory politics. I believe this draws attention to a certain complacency in conventional political theory. Generally such political theory concentrates on the question of how to bring into being the one, or single, successful civil society. Each political philosopher might have his own prescription as to how this might occur but the objective is the same: how to create a working political order. In this respect, a great deal of political theory has not changed from the time of Plato and Aristotle. Just as Plato and Aristotle sought to discern in, respectively, *The Republic* and *Politics*, what was the ideal form for the domestic political system, so most political theorists are currently occupied with depicting the ideal internal order.

We might see this preoccupation as analogous with the concerns of those occupied by the academic study of the modern family. A contemporary sociologist whose interest is in the family might well believe that there are enormous difficulties in putting together a persuasive view of family relations. If there is now an ideal of the family it must, in western societies, have undergone considerable alteration in the course of the twentieth century.

Controversies will doubtlessly abound as to whether or not, for instance, a one-parent family functions successfully. However, once sociologists of the family have put forward their view of the most suitable family structure they might well believe their job was done. From my perspective this would not be a very subtle conclusion to draw. The more sophisticated family sociologist will see that the family falls into the wider context of the society. Thus we would expect that a persuasive account of the modern family would be one which would also evince a convincing view of modern society.

Just as the embeddedness of the family in society is important for the study of the family in contemporary society, so the embeddedness of the national state in the international political order is vital for the study of political theory. It is not persuasive nowadays for political theorists to put forward an account of the best form of the state without regard to the interstate context. Habermas shows an awareness of this, not so much in the attention he gives to international issues in his political theory but rather in the attention he gives to the fluidity and incompleteness of legislation and policy at the national level.

Public law within the state is conditioned for Habermas by a continuous debate. In a democratic society this debate is open, with each citizen potentially taking part. Law is positive (and has, therefore, to be obeyed) but it is normatively grounded. As good citizens we conform to the law, but the law emanates from the autonomous choices and discourse of the citizens themselves. We obey those rules we ourselves shape. Over time those rules may be seen as fluid, although at any point in time they are set. Morality and legality are mutually conditioning. Law is the public codification of the moral deliberations of citizens concerning their external actions, and morality is enhanced and (often) realized by the existence of publicly enforced law.

The separate and distinct contribution which morality makes to the development and existence of law has important implications in the international sphere. The lack of an agreed sovereign political authority in international society cannot be cited as a sufficient reason for the absence of law. Natural law theorists, like Grotius and Locke, have a point. Law arises from the ethical discourse of people. International law arises from the same discourse, but here it is also a discourse on peoples (among one another in mutual bilateral contact with one another, and in international institutions). Domestic lawmaking for Habermas in a democratic society gives rise to rules which are subject to continuous alteration and amendment. Thus, that the rules of present international law are not fixed (nor wholly binding) is not of itself a barrier to the recognition of international law.

Habermas's discourse ethics approach to the making of law raises the possibility of the universalization of the law of democratic states. Or, conversely, we might say that present international law, in so far as it is founded in a morality amongst states and their citizens, provides the possibility of a law-governed international order. But it is important to bear in mind that sovereign domestic political authority plays a key role for Habermas in the discourse ethics view of law. International anarchy will not bring law. In the absence of a central authority which can act as a sovereign we have to rely upon the existing sovereign bodies in world society (states) to act in harmony with those international institutions which presently exist, such as the UN, to bring about the observance of law. But since all sovereign authority rests upon a prior, working, ethical community, any world sovereign authority can only be the expression of the requirements and needs of the world's citizens. Habermas's account of law making in a democratic state is one telling example of political theory which takes us beyond the boundaries of states.

Speculation about the political arrangements of the country in which one lives is a natural starting point for political theory. It is a point of orientation of overwhelming value, but it is one that can be profitably extended to include the wider world. That this is not simply the esoteric demand of a political philosopher or the special pleading of international relations specialists can be seen from this excerpt from a recent North American textbook by R. B. Fowler and J. R. Orenstein, *An Introduction to Political Theory*: 'As scholars and citizens, political theorists need to learn more about the processes of international political conflict in order to prescribe values and systems that either strengthen existing peaceful institutions or advocate their transcendence where necessary. Political theory as a discipline needs to deal with universal values that are large enough to deflect the dangers that modern military technology and the threat of war have wrought. Only if such issues are ameliorated (if they cannot be solved) can political theory turn its full attention to other issues of human potential that are not eroded by the opportunity costs and threats of war-and-peace issues in the nuclear age.'[1] The essays in this book represent an attempt to realize in practice this general aim.

NOTES

1. R. B. Fowler and J. R. Orenstein, *An Introduction to Political Theory*, HarperCollins, New York, 1993

Bibliography

LIST OF WORKS CITED

Ackerman, B., *Social Justice in the Liberal State*, Yale University Press, New Haven, 1980

Ansell-Pearson, K., *Nietzsche contra Rousseau*, Cambridge, 1991

Aristotle, *Politics*, Penguin, Harmondsworth, 1970

Avineri, S., *Hegel's Theory of the Modern State*, Cambridge, 1972

Ball, T. and Dagger, R., *Political Ideologies and the Democratic Ideal*, HarperCollins, New York, 1995

Barry, N. P., *An Introduction to Modern Political Theory*, Macmillan, London, 1989

Beitz, C., *Political Theory and International Relations*, Princeton University Press, New Jersey, 1979

Berlin, I., *Four Essays on Liberty*, Oxford, 1975

Bromley, D. W., *Environment and Economy*, Blackwell, Oxford, 1991

Buchanan, A., *Marxism and Justice*, Rowman and Littlefield, New Jersey, 1982

Bull, H., Kingsbury, B. and Roberts, A., *Hugo Grotius and International Relations*, Oxford University Press, Oxford, 1992

Buckle, S., *Natural Law and the Theory of Property*, Oxford University Press, Oxford, 1991

Burke, E., *Reflections on the French Revolution*, Penguin, Harmondsworth, 1973

Burns, J. H., *The Cambridge History of Political Thought*, Cambridge University Press, Cambridge, 1994

Butterfield, H. and Wight, M. (eds), *Diplomatic Investigations*, Allen & Unwin, London, 1966

Cox, R. H., *Locke on War and Peace*, Oxford University Press, Oxford, 1960

Despland, M., *Kant on History and Religion*, McGill/Queen's University Press, Montreal and Hegel, London, 1973

Edwards, C. S., *Hugo Grotius: The Miracle of Holland*, Nelson Hall, Chicago, 1981

Eliade, M., *Encyclopedia of Religion*, Macmillan, New York, 1987

Finnis, J., *Studies in Political Thought from Gerson to Grotius, 1414–1625*, Cambridge University Press, Cambridge, 1922

Freeden, M., *Rights*, Open University Press, Buckingham, 1991

Gauthier, D. P., *The Logic of Leviathan*, Oxford University Press, Oxford, 1979

Giddens, A., *The Consequences of Modernity*, Polity Press, Oxford, 1990

Gramsci, A., *Prison Notebooks*, Lawrence & Wishart, London, 1976

Grant, R., *John Locke's Liberalism*, Chicago University Press, Chicago, 1987

Grotius, H., *De Jure Belli ac Pacis Libri Tres* (tr. F. W. Kelley), Oceania Publications, New York, 1964

Haakonssen, K., 'Hugo Grotius and the History of Political Thought', *Political Theory*, 13, No. 2, 1985, 239–65

Habermas, J., *Faktizität und Geltung: Beiträge zur Diskurstheorie des Rechts und des demokratischen Rechtsstaats*, Suhrkamp, Frankfurt am Mein, 1992

Hall, D., *Puritanism in Seventeenth-Century Massachusetts*, Holt Rinehart and Winston, New York 1988

Hampsher-Monk, I., *A History of Modern Political Thought*, Blackwell, Oxford, 1992

Hampton, J. *Hobbes and the Social Contract Tradition*, Cambridge University Press, Cambridge, 1990

Hegel, G. W. F., *Philosophy of History*, Dover, New York, 1956

Hegel, G. W. F., *Philosophy of Right*, Oxford University Press, Oxford, 1969

Hegel, G. W. F., *Science of Logic*, Allen & Unwin, London, 1969

Held, D., *Models of Democracy*, Polity Press, Oxford, 1987

Held, D., *Political Theory Today*, Polity Press, Oxford, 1991

Held, D., *Prospects for Democracy*, Polity Press, Oxford, 1992

Hobbes, T., *Leviathan*, Fontana, London, 1969

Hoffman, S. and Fidler, D. (eds), *Rousseau on International Relations*, Oxford University Press, 1991

Hollingdale, R. J., *Nietzsche Reader*, Penguin, Harmondsworth, 1977

Kant, I., *Critique of Practical Reason* (tr. L. W. Beck), Macmillan, London, 1988

Kant, I., *Metaphysics of Morals* (tr. M. Gregor), Cambridge, 1992

Kant, I., *Lectures on Logic*, Cambridge University Press, Cambridge, 1992

Kant, I., 'Perpetual Peace', in *Kant Selections* (ed. L. W. Beck), London/New York, 1988

Kant, I., *Religion within the Limits of Pure Reason Alone* (tr. T. M. Greene and H. Hoyt), Harper, New York, 1960

Lenin, V. I., *Imperialism*, Progress Publishers, Moscow, 1971

Lively, J., *Democracy*, Blackwell, Oxford, 1975

Locke, J., *Essays on the Law of Nature* (tr. and ed. W. Von Leyden), Oxford University Press, Oxford, 1970

Locke, J., *Two Treatises of Government*, Dent, London, 1977

Lukes, S., *Marxism and Morality*, Oxford University Press, Oxford, 1985

Macfarlane, L., *The Theory and Practice of Human Rights*, Maurice Temple Smith, London, 1985

Machiavelli, N., *The Prince*, Penguin, Harmondsworth, 1968

Marx, K. and Engels, F., *Communist Manifesto*, Progress Publishers, Moscow, 1969

Mill, James, *Essay on Government* (ed. J. Lively and J. Rees), Oxford University Press, Oxford, 1978

Mill, J. S., *On Liberty*, Oxford University Press, Oxford, 1987

Morgenthau, H., *Politics Among Nations*, Knopf, New York, 1973

Morison, W. L., *John Austin*, Edward Arnold, London, 1982

Nehemas, A., *Nietzsche: Life as Literature*, Harvard University Press, Cambridge, Mass., 1985

Nietzsche, *Beyond Good and Evil*, Penguin, Harmondsworth, 1988

Nietzsche, *Werke in sechs Bänden* Vol.2, Carl Hanser Verlag, Munchen/Wein, 1980

Nozick, R., *Anarchy, State and Utopia*, Blackwell, Oxford, 1974

Pangle, T. L., *The Spirit of Modern Republicanism: The Moral Vision of the American Founders and the philosophy of Locke*, Chicago University Press, Chicago, 1988

Pelczynski, Z. A. (ed.), *Hegel's Political Writings*, Oxford University Press, Oxford, 1969

Pelczynski, Z. A. (ed.), *The State and Civil Society*, Cambridge University Press, Cambridge, 1984

Plant, R., *Modern Political Theory*, Blackwell, Oxford, 1991

Plato, *The Republic*, Penguin, Harmondsworth, 1970

Pogge, T. W., *Realizing Rawls*, Cornell University Press, New York, 1989

Raphael, D. D., *Problems of Political Philosophy*, Macmillan, London, 1990

Rawls, J., *A Theory of Justice*, Oxford University Press, Oxford, 1972

Rawls, J., 'The Law of Peoples', in Shute, S. and Hurley, S., *On Human Rights*, Basic Books, New York and London, 1994

Raz, J., *The Morality of Freedom*, Oxford University Press, Oxford, 1986

Reiss, H., Kant's Political Writings (tr. H. Nisbet), Cambridge University Press, Cambridge, 1977

Rosenau, J., *Turbulence in World Politics*, Princeton University Press, New Jersey, 1990

Sartre, J.-P., *Critique of Dialectical Reason*, Verso, London, 1982

Taylor, C., *Sources of the Self*, Cambridge University Press, Cambridge, 1979

Tuck, R., *Natural Rights Theories: Their Origin and Development*, Cambridge University Press, Cambridge, 1979

Tully, J., *An Approach to Political Philosophy: Locke in Contexts*, Cambridge University Press, Cambridge, 1993

Van der Linden, H., *Kantian Ethics and Socialism*, Hackett, Indianapolis and London, 1988

Vansomeren, L., *Umpire to the Nations*, Dennis Dobson, London, 1965

Vincent, A., *Modern Political Ideologies*, Blackwell, Oxford, 1992,

Vincent, R. J., *Human Rights and International Relations*, Cambridge University Press, Cambridge, 1986,

Waltz, K., *Man, the State and War*, Columbia University Press, New York, 1959

Warren, M., *Nietzsche and Political Thought*, M.I.T. Press, Cambridge, Mass., 1988

Webb, C., *Kant's Philosophy of Religion*, Oxford University Press, Oxford, 1926

Weber, M., *The Protestant Ethic and the Spirit of Capitalism* (tr. T. Parsons), Unwin, London, 1984

Williams, H., Wright, M., Evans, A., *A Reader in International Politics and Political Theory*, Open University Press, Buckingham, 1991

Williams, H., *Concepts of Ideology*, Wheatsheaf Books, Brighton, 1988

Williams, H., *International Relations in Political Theory*, Open University Press, Milton Keynes, 1991

Williams, H., *Kant's Political Philosophy*, Blackwell, Oxford, 1983

Wood, Allen, *Kant's Rational Theology*, Cornell University Press, New York, 1978

Yasuaki, O., *A Normative Approach to War: Peace, War and Justice in Hugo Grotius*, Oxford University Press, Oxford, 1993

OTHER WORKS

Aron, R., *Peace and War* (tr. R. Howard, A. Fox), Anchor, New York, 1973

Beitz, C. R., *Political Theory and International Relations*, Princeton University Press, New Jersey, 1979

Brown, P. G., Shue, H., *Boundaries: National autonomy and its limits*, Rowman & Littlefield, New York, 1981

Donelan, M., *The Reason of States*, Allen & Unwin, London, 1978

Donelan, M., *Elements of International Political Theory*, Clarendon, Oxford, 1993

Forbes, I., Hoffman, M., *International Relations, Political Theory and the Ethics of Intervention*, Macmillan, Basingstoke

Hoffman, S., *Contemporary Theory in International Relations*, Greenwood Press, Conn., 1977

Holsti, K. J., *The Dividing discipline: Hegemony and Diversity in International Theory*, Allen & Unwin, Boston, 1985

Jacobson, Norman, *Pride and Solace: the Functions and Limits of Political Theory*, Methuen, New York, 1986

Kubalkova, V., *Marxism-Leninism and Theory of International Relations*, Routledge, London, 1980

Linklater, A., *Beyond Realism and Marxism*, Macmillan, Basingstoke, 1990

Linklater, A., *Men and Citizens in the Theory of International Relations*, Macmillan, London, 1990

Mayall, J., *The Community of States: A Study in International Political Theory*, Allen & Unwin, London, 1982

Midgley, Ernest, *The Natural Law Tradition and the Theory of International Relations*, Elek, London, 1975

Rengger, N. J., Hoffman, M., *Beyond the Inter-Paradigm Debate: Critical Theory and International Relations*, Harvester Wheatsheaf, Hemel Hempstead, 1990

Rosenau, James N., *The Adaption of National Societies: A Theory of Political System Behaviour and Transformation*, McCaleb-Seiler, 1970

Rosenberg, J., *The Empire of Civil Society: a Critique of the Realist Theory of International Relations*, Verso, London, 1993

Rothstein, R. L., *The Evolution of Theory in International Relations*, University of South Carolina Press, 1991

Skidmore, Hudson, *The Limits of State Autonomy: Societal Groups and Foreign Policy Formulation*, Westview Press, Boulder, 1993

Sylvester, Christine, *Feminist Theory and International Relations Theory in a Postmodern Era*, Cambridge University Press, Cambridge, 1993

Thompson, K. W., *Traditions and Values in Politics and Diplomacy*, Louisiana State University Press, Louisiana, 1992

Walker, R. B. J., *Inside/Outside: International Relations as Political Theory*, Cambridge University Press, Cambridge, 1993

Waltz, K. N., *Theory of International Politics*, McGraw-Hill, London, 1979

Young, O. R., *Compliance and Public Authority*, Johns Hopkins University Press, Baltimore, 1979

Index